THE *EXPO* FILES

AND OTHER ARTICLES BY
THE CRUSADING JOURNALIST

STIEG LARSSON

*Translated from the Swedish
by Laurie Thompson*

Edited by Daniel Poohl

With an Introduction by Tariq Ali

MacLehose Press

MacLehose Press
An imprint of Quercus
New York • London

© 2011 by Stieg Larsson/Expo
Published by agreement with Norstedts Agency
English translation © 2012 by Laurie Thompson
Introduction © 2012 by Tariq Ali
First published in Sweden as *En annan sida av Stieg Larsson* by
Expo in 2011
First published in the United States by Quercus in 2014

Any member of educational institutions wishing to photocopy part or
all of the work for classroom use or anthology should send inquiries to
Permissions c/o Quercus Publishing Inc., 31 West 57th Street, 6th Floor,
New York, NY 10019, or to permissions@quercus.com.

ISBN 978-1-62365-064-3

Library of Congress Control Number: 2013937745

Distributed in the United States and Canada by
Random House Publisher Services
c/o Random House, 1745 Broadway
New York, NY 10019

Manufactured in the United States

2 4 6 8 10 9 7 5 3 1

www.quercus.com

CONTENTS

Preface: Another side of Stieg Larsson—a voice sadly missed   3

Introduction by Tariq Ali   9

Terror killings can happen in Stockholm (*Expo*—1995)   17

The new popular movement (*Expo/Svartvitt*—1999)   29

Democracy in Europe? (*Expo*—2003)   41

Living with Pia Kjaersgaard (*Expo*—2002)   45

The return of anti-Semitism (*Expo/Monitor*—1998)   55

The world picture of superstition (*Internationalen*—1983)   67

A defeat for democracy (*Expo*, previously unpublished)   75

Response to anti-democratic propaganda
    (*Expo*—2002, with Mikael Ekman)   81

Cracks behind a unified façade (www.expo.se—2003)   91

The party that's over the limit (www.expo.se—2003)   97

The Sweden Democrats and their defector
    (www.expo.se—2004)   103

N.D. sidelined (www.expo.se—2004)   111

An attack on democracy (www.expo.se—2003)   119

Dear *Expo* . . . (www.expo.se—2003)   125

The intellectual breakdown of *Expressen*
    (www.expo.se—2003)   131

The pea-brains of nationalism (www.expo.se—2004)   137

"The world's most dangerous profession"
    (From the book *Överleva deadline*)   143

Gang rape as racist propaganda (www.expo.se—2003)   157

Exit Paulsson (www.expo.se—2004)   161

Swedish and un-Swedish violence towards women
    (From the book *Debatten om hedersmord*)   169

Terror aimed at homosexuals (*Expo*—1997)   203

The assault on Facundo Unia (www.expo.se—2003)   209

The terror we turn a blind eye to (*Expo*—2003)   217

Svenska Motståndsrörelsen (Swedish Resistance Movement)
    —a Zionist conspiracy? (www.expo.se—2003)   221

9,001 kilometres to Beijing (*Vagabond*—1987)   227

Biographies   247

Numbers in the text throughout the book refer to the explanatory notes at the end of several of the articles.

PREFACE

Another side of Stieg Larsson
—a voice sadly missed

As time passes, memories of my colleague and friend Stieg begin to fade. I recall the smoke-laden atmosphere in the coffee room where we discussed the latest developments in far-right movements, and listened to Stieg's endless repertoire of anecdotes. About his National Service, his time at T.T. (Tidningarnas Telegrambyrå—the Swedish Central News Agency), his trips to Africa. But I have trouble in remembering everything that was said.

But I do remember one thing perfectly clearly.

His way of writing. How he would bang his fingers down hard on the keyboard, fast and accurately, as if he were still using a typewriter.

Stieg was often stressed. A small office with so much to do. He was happy to delegate, but even so usually wanted to keep a finger in the pie. He was always adjusting the texts one last time, checking the editing one last time, correcting the reports one last time.

Yet somehow or other, he always looked relaxed as he sat there, typing away.

He often squandered hours by writing long e-mails to right-wing extremists who were eager to set debates in motion. The explanatory notes and handbooks he wrote for new members of staff were immaculately formulated, informative and comprehensive. One year he kept the editorial board entertained by circulating a series of summer updates via e-mail. He wrote polemical articles, books, pamphlets, policy documents.

And he wrote crime novels.

Stieg knew his crime novels were good. He stated quite early on, somewhat cockily, that they were going to be his pension. But nobody could possibly have dreamed they would turn out to be as successful as they have been. There is no getting away from the fact that the story of Lisbeth Salander and Mikael Blomkvist has knocked the rest of Stieg's writing into the shade.

This book is intended to remind readers of the other side of Stieg Larsson's writing. To some extent it helps to explain what Stieg wanted to say in his Millennium Trilogy. It is not possible to separate the novels from his commitment to opposing racism and promoting women's rights. The book also provides information about Stieg

Larsson the journalist, and the issues to which he devoted his life.

What you are about to read is far from everything that Stieg the journalist wrote. He was a contributor to various books, and for many years was a correspondent for the English journal *Searchlight*, besides being a contributor to other magazines.

Included here is some travel writing and several articles he wrote while working for the Swedish Central News Agency. They demonstrate that for Stieg his writing was about more than just expounding political ideas. He also wrote because he enjoyed doing so. Most of the articles are taken from the first ten years of *Expo*. They comprise columns, leading articles and correspondence with readers. Some of the texts selected are extracts from books that in various ways touched on subjects close to his heart. The articles are arranged thematically, and provide a guide to Stieg's views on anti-racist and feminist questions. At the same time they highlight a worrying political development.

When the journal *Expo* was launched in the mid-1990s, the violent neo-Nazi movement was attracting a great deal of attention in Sweden. The anti-immigration policies of New Democracy[1] resulted in the party's resignation from the Swedish parliament, and the so-called nationalist movement made its presence felt by a series of murders and dramatic white-power concerts.

During the first ten years of the twenty-first century, the spotlight focused on the Sweden Democrats[2] and, in the early days, the National Democrats[3]—parties with roots in the murky sludge that was beginning to ooze into democratically elected institutions.

In the most recent elections, the Sweden Democrats won seats in parliament. Previously regarded as political clowns, they had now entered the corridors of power.

With hindsight it is easy to see that the driving forces behind Stieg's crime novels are also present in the rest of his writing. He had a broad basic education. He could be sarcastic and confrontational. He did not hesitate to make fun of the marginalized white-power movement's peculiar way of life and conspiratorial philosophy.

I was never especially interested in Stieg's crime novels while he was writing them. Strictly in order to be polite, I once asked him how he would exploit the fame he hoped to achieve with them. The plan was well mapped out in his head. The financial security they would provide would enable him to spend all his time writing even more crime novels, polemical articles and columns.

Obviously, what I miss most is Stieg the man. His humor, his drive, his generosity. But I am also sad that he was not able to experience his success. Not for the success in itself, but for the possibilities it would have opened up for him.

He would have had a lot to say now. About the increase in Islamophobia. About the progress achieved by the Sweden Democrats. About the violence that men inflict upon women. About issues he never had the opportunity to explore while he was working on *Expo*.

The world has become a little quieter without Stieg around.

This is our way of giving him a voice again. Our way of making sure that his thumping away at the keyboard was not in vain.

Daniel Poohl

Notes

1. New Democracy, a populist party with a xenophobic agenda, was very successful in the first half of the 1990s. The party was founded in 1991, and that same year entered the Swedish parliament with 6.7 percent of the vote. During their time in parliament the party was beset by internal battles and lost its seats in the 1994 general election.
2. Sweden Democrats was a nationalist right-wing populist party formed in 1988. Several of its founders had a background of involvement with fascist and Nazi organizations. Today, the party has twenty seats in parliament, having received 5.7 percent of the vote in the parliamentary elections in 2010.
3. National Democrats was a right-wing party with close ties to the Swedish Nazi movement. The party was founded as a radical breakaway from the Sweden Democrats in 2001. In the parliamentary elections of 2010, the National Democrats won three communal seats and got 1,141 votes.

Introduction

Stieg Larsson's continuous battle against right-wing extremism and the security and police establishments of his country is the central fact of his literary and political biography.
The issues he raised and the positions he defended are even
more important now than they were during his lifetime.
They touch the mainsprings of European political and cultural life today. Larsson is sometimes portrayed as a writer
with a heart deeply touched by sadness, even despair. Not
true. His sensitivity to the oppression of women and the
prejudice against immigrants made him angry, sometimes
to the point of irrationality, but he never despaired. For

him it was too passive an emotion. His "crime novels" are engaged, bitter and savage in their portraits of the enemy. As a lifelong socialist (and, for a period, a Trotskyist), he wanted to change the world, but was aware that this was not an individual task and always worked with groups and in circles to help maximize his political effectiveness.

His concerns and compassions were straightforward and should not be interpreted as melancholy. His journalism, as is obvious from this collection of texts, was driven by a hatred of all prejudice based on gender, race or class. He despised Swedish chauvinism. All this is gleaned from his works. I never met him, although am told by friends that Stieg and his partner Eva Gabrielsson attended some of my talks in Sweden in the '70s: I visited the country regularly during that decade. What is refreshing about these articles is the tone. There is no whingeing from Larsson. His political essays reflect a cold anger.

He grew up in postwar Sweden during the Cold War. Every Swedish family was aware of the depths to which its elite had sunk during the Second World War, when it collaborated in a wholehearted fashion with the Third Reich under a national government led by Social Democrats. It was certainly not their finest hour, but they perfected the art of subservience to a power without being militarily occupied, echoes of which have become only too visible in recent years. The monarch himself was sympathetic to Hitler's cause (his personal physician vetoed giving refuge to several German-Jewish doctors, with dire consequences) and the University of Lund invited Joseph Goebbels in order to honor him. They were spared the disgrace. Goebbels declined the invitation. The Scandinavian joke—it took several weeks for the Germans to take Norway, a day to occupy Denmark and a telephone call to take Sweden—is based on reality. The memory of this was officially erased after the war, but not for everyone. The main opposition during the war had come from the Communist Party. This gave it an aura that benefited the left as a whole.

Stieg Larsson's so-called "obsession" with the Swedish far right was not at all misplaced. Like many on the left, he knew that fascist ideology had penetrated deep and left an oppressive strain even in the mainstream of Swedish political culture. He was prescient in this regard. I thought of him after the 2010 election results in Sweden, when the sanitized fascists won parliamentary representation. With 5.7 percent of the vote they now had twenty members of parliament. Their campaign had played to old prejudices. A newly elected member, Kent Ekeroth, stoked Islamophobia just as their forebears had once lit the fires of anti-Semitism: "If Sweden had a majority of Muslims who wanted sharia law, what do you think would happen?"

As Daniel Poohl of *Expo* wrote: "The Sweden Democrats were able to say to Swedes that the problems they see in society and the problems that they have personally are directly linked to immigration. And those who ended up voting for the S. D. believed in what the party was saying."

The founder of the magazine had already predicted this development:

The equation was simple: in order to achieve political success the Sweden Democrats needed to acquire support from voters who were dissatisfied with the political establishment, but did not consider themselves to be Nazis or "nationalists." As long as the S.D. appeared to be a traditional Nazi organization with skinheads and uniformed lunatics to the fore, the party scared off all potential voters. When Mikael Jansson took over as leader in 1995, one of his first actions was to ban the wearing of uniforms at public meetings. Since then the party has gradually sidelined the most obvious madmen and militants and replaced them with elegantly dressed and comparatively house-trained activists, including both young people and pensioners. The crudest racial propaganda has been toned down . . .

Fascist propaganda works best on the fears of the weak, but its successes depend on what is happening in society as a whole. An economic downturn coupled with the widespread Islamophobia that emanates from mainstream politics is a poisonous combination, currently being utilized by far-right groups throughout the Western world. So deep does it go that when a right-wing extremist kills and maims, the first reaction of the media networks is to assume that the perpetrator is a Muslim. This was already the case in 1995 when Timothy McVeigh bombed the Federal Building in Oklahoma. Before his identity was known the local media reported "swarthy, Arab-looking types" who had been seen in the vicinity. It was pure fantasy.

In his description and analysis of that terrorist attack, Larsson insisted that it was shortsighted to view the event as the act of a lone killer or madman. There was always, he argued, "a political and historical explanation." He would not have been at all surprised by the events of July 2011 in neighboring Norway, when a homegrown terrorist, Anders Behring Breivik, butchered dozens of young people. This time the media and Western leaders assumed it was a Muslim attack because of Norwegian involvement in the Afghanistan war. Messages of support poured in from Obama and his E.U. followers. Dark-skinned Norwegian citizens were jostled and attacked on the streets of Oslo before the identity of the terrorist was revealed. Silence followed. The votaries of Western civilization had nothing more to say. A terror attack was suddenly transformed into "a national tragedy." Breivik was a madman. But as the Norwegian writer Aslak Sira Myhre pointed out in the *Guardian* the day after, it was not so simple. The terrorist was not a Muslim but a Muslim-hater, an Islamophobe whose manifesto revealed close reading of columnists in Europe's mainstream newspapers. Myhre wrote in very Larsson-like tones:

> Anyone who has glanced at the web pages of racist groups or followed the online debates of Norwegian newspapers will have seen the rage with which Islamophobia is being spread; the poisonous hatred with which anonymous writers sting anti-racist liberals and the left is only too visible. The July 22 terrorist has participated in many such debates. He has been an active member of one of the biggest Norwegian political parties, the populist right party, until 2006. He left them and sought his ideology instead among the community of anti-Islamist groups on the internet.

With the attacks on immigrants and travelling people reaching new heights—the burning of travelling people in

Naples, mass deportations in France, brutal evictions in Britain and Spain—were Larsson's concerns all that far-fetched? He knew that for the most oppressed layers in society it can be a colossal effort to live. The hard silence of official justice annoyed him just as much as judicial misdemeanors, cover-ups, a refusal to face facts. Stieg Larsson would not remain calm in the face of political evil. Here he reminds me of another Swedish non-conformist, to put it no stronger.

Long before the ignominy of the Second World War, another radical Swedish writer had lambasted the national traditions of his country. August Strindberg, who died in 1912, challenged the false and fraudulent accounts of the Swedish bourgeoisie. His first novel, *The Red Room*, was a devastating satire on the corruptions of capitalism and the hypocrisies of bourgeois life. In a set of acute essays, Strindberg exposed the pretensions of the national culture, its religion (his book containing a short story that rudely mocked the Holy Communion was banned), gender inequalities and the official histories of the time. The reaction was bitter and brutal, compelling the writer to leave his country. Like Larsson after him, Strindberg never compromised his integrity. His motto was simple but effective: never write to please. That way lies failure. He was never a writer desperate for honors or prizes or to reach an accommodation with the much-despised rulers of his country in order to gain recognition. He spat on people like that, once or twice literally, if the stories are to be believed. He challenged them with real passion, and their primitive and simplistic defenders made fools of themselves as they attempted to destroy the playwright's literary and personal reputation. Strindberg's supporters raised thousands of kronor and presented him with the anti-Nobel Prize for literature.

Stieg Larsson has become a posthumous global cult. His books are translated into all the major languages and not a few minor ones. Were he still alive he would have been self-mocking and taken the fame in his stride, but the money that his books are earning would have been used mainly to support the causes that he defended all his life: investigative journalism, anti-racist and anti-fascist movements and journals, the struggle for democracy and social justice worldwide. This book provides a glimpse of Larsson denied to most readers of his novels. It is not that his politics are absent in the latter. If anything the contrary, but the clarity of his non-fiction writings enhances his stature and they deserve to be read by his admiring fans. It will educate them and, who knows, even push them in the direction of activism. Larsson would have loved that . . .

Tariq Ali, October 2011

TERROR KILLINGS CAN HAPPEN IN STOCKHOLM

Expo no. 1—1995

More than 170 dead and 450 injured, many of them seriously—that was the result of the terrorist attack in Oklahoma City a few weeks ago.[1] Unfortunately the indications are that a similar terrorist attack could take place in Sweden.

The Oklahoma City massacre was no natural catastrophe; it was meticulously planned and deliberately implemented mass murder. In the aftermath, America is fumbling around groggily, searching for explanations. But American researchers who have been studying right-wing extremism were not particularly surprised by the attack. On the contrary, for them the question was not *if* an Oklahoma massacre would take place, but *when*.

The bombing in Oklahoma has a political and historical explanation.

Political breakthrough

In the United States of America, as in Sweden, fascist and openly anti-democratic groups have never achieved a political breakthrough on a national scale. The biggest far-right organization in the U.S.A. was traditionally the Ku Klux Klan, which amassed three million members in the early twentieth century. The Klan's message can be summed up as "hate politics." Their activities were basically attacks on various "enemies"—primarily blacks, Jews, liberals and Catholics, but also women's liberation, industrial capitalism, working-class movements, and so on.

The original Klan was not an out-and-out fascist organization of the type that sprang up in Europe, but rather a reactionary and violent protest movement nourished by social unrest and populism—a sort of armed Swedish New Democracy, if you like. During its existence the Klan carried out political murders, terrorist attacks and several thousand lynchings in the South and Mid-West.

Hitler's Germany

The Klan could have become stabilized as a far-right power base had it not made the mistake of embracing Hitlerite Germany in the 1930s and aligning itself with Nazism. In only a few years the Klan lost most of its popular support, and since the Second World War it has seldom been able to amass more than a few tens of thousand activists.

After the war the fascist tradition in the U.S.A.—as in Sweden—went into hibernation as an isolated and politically insignificant movement. The far right created a sort of political parallel universe that could be characterized by irrational conspiracy theories. Paradoxically, the very isolation and lack of popular support have resulted in the creation of an increasingly desperate sect mentality.

Since the end of the 1970s, right-wing extremism has once more been raising its ugly head. A new generation of activists nurtured by the sects has now entered the stage. Unlike their predecessors they are not lynch mobs armed with shotguns, but a semi-professional army with automatic rifles and heavy military equipment.

Aryan Nations

One cornerstone of the far right is the neo-Nazi organization Aryan Nations, which came into being in the early 1980s. Aryan Nations maintain that the U.S.A. is occupied by Z.O.G., an abbreviation of "Zionist Occupation Government," which they say is a "Jewish conspiracy" that controls the government and state authorities. They claim that Z.O.G.'s aim is to eliminate the white Aryan race by encouraging interracial cross-breeding. Z.O.G. is also accused of introducing more restrictive weapons legislation with the aim of disarming the white race. In order to protect itself the white race is forced to conduct a war on several fronts. First, the enemy number one, Z.O.G.—the F.B.I. and the U.S. government—must be defeated in a civil war. And then

Jews and non-white races must be removed from the face of the earth.

Crazy? Of course, but it is for that reason that a federal building in Oklahoma is a target for American racists.

Formally, Aryan Nations disguise themselves as a Free Church. Their headquarters is at Hayden Lake in the state of Idaho, in the sparsely populated northwest of the U.S.A. But, as everybody realizes, it is different from normal Free Churches. Their chapel is a sort of bunker policed by armed guards who patrol the surrounding area. Instead of a crucifix, a portrait of Adolf Hitler hangs over their altar.

Crazy or not, for a short period at the beginning of the 1980s this was the fastest-growing Free Church in the whole of the U.S.A. At its height it had over fifty parishes with up to fifty thousand adherents. One reason for its expansion was that it was able to attract extremists from a wide variety of groups—the Ku Klux Klan, traditional Nazis, survivalists and paramilitary groups, certain right-wing anarchist associations and several more: there was room for all of them under the Aryan Nations umbrella.

The "church" educates its initiates in the politics of hatred. The enemies are Jews and the proponents of mixed-race crossbreeding. The worst sin a white Aryan can commit is to enter into a sexual relationship with a partner from a different race; this crime is punishable by the death penalty. The movement organizes seminars and study circles. The literature they favor—in addition to such classics as *Mein Kampf* and *The Protocols of the Elders of Zion*— comprises books that encourage armed conflict and guerrilla warfare against governments, Jews and black people.

Other books they study describe in detail how to conduct such warfare.

A typical example is the novel *The Turner Diaries*, which attracted attention after the Oklahoma massacre. The book describes a fictional white resistance movement—the Order—that fights its crusade by means of assassinations and atrocities on an escalating scale. Ten pages of the book describe in detail how the Order destroys a federal building, an F.B.I. headquarters.

This is how it is done: pack forty-five sacks of fertilizer—ammonium nitrate—into the back of a van. The contents of each sack are mixed with about one liter of engine oil, which results in an explosive compound of devastating strength. In order to trigger the explosion they use plastic explosive paste attached to a delayed-action bomb. They then park the van and walk away. The attack results in the death of seven hundred people. A "victory" in the fight against Z.O.G.

The bomb described in *The Turner Diaries* corresponds exactly to the one used in Oklahoma City. One does not have to be clairvoyant to suspect that the perpetrators had studied *The Turner Diaries*.

The book was published in 1978 and became a bestseller among extremists all over the world. Sales have been estimated at more than 250,000 copies. Among the readers are Swedish neo-Nazis.

The armed wing

There is a democratic problem associated with this type of literature. It is not forbidden to write, read or possess offensive books. Nor is it forbidden to fantasize about genocide.

If these lunatics were content to sit in their bunkers and dream about massacres, we would have no need to pay them any attention. But, unfortunately, they do not content themselves with that.

In 1982 a paramilitary group was formed in the U.S.A. that functioned as the armed wing of the Aryan Nations. The squad, which had about two hundred members, was known as the Silent Brotherhood. The F.B.I. did not beat about the bush but called them the Order, the name of the fictional group in *The Turner Diaries*. Undeclared war was launched in 1983, in accordance with the guiding principles laid down in the handbook. A war chest was accumulated, thanks to a series of armed robberies. A death list of "enemies" was drawn up. The best known victim was the Jewish broadcaster Alan Berg, who was gunned down with an automatic weapon outside his home in Denver, Colorado, in 1984.

For a short time in 1984 the Order was the object of the biggest police hunt in the U.S.A. since the murder of President Kennedy. More than one hundred members were arrested. Two activists, David Lane and Bruce Carroll Pierce, were sentenced for the murder of Alan Berg to 160 and 250 years in prison respectively. Others received prison sentences ranging from thirty to ninety years for conspiracy to murder.

The leader of the Order, Robert Jay Mathews, was never brought to court. He barricaded himself into his bunker and was killed after a 48-hour gun battle with the F.B.I. Since then he has been one of the most notorious martyrs of neo-Nazism.

The imprisonment of members of the Order was a setback for Aryan Nations, but the ones sentenced were only the foot soldiers. The instigators, the ideologues who created the basis for the movement by preaching racial hatred, anti-Semitic conspiracy theories and armed rebellion against the American government, were acquitted. For the same reason it will be difficult ever to pin down and punish those responsible for the Oklahoma massacre, even if the bombers confess. There is simply not enough proof.

Since the members of the Order were arrested, the ideologues have calmly continued to build up the organizations they hope will be at the core of the battle against Jews and black people. For several years they have been concentrating their attention on the so-called Militia Movement, which attracts common-or-garden paranoiacs, dissatisfied conservatives and weapons freaks. The Militia Movement contains precisely the kind of idiots that the Aryan Nations know are receptive to more extreme manifestos.

There are no legal methods available to come to grips with the Aryan Nations. The very constitution that the far right is fighting to demolish gives them the right to form organizations such as theirs. They have plenty of money, comprehensive propaganda outlets, a well-organized cadre of activists, and access to weapons.

It is tempting to conclude that there is something fundamentally wrong with the American system that passively allows the formation of hate-filled racist groups and heavily armed paramilitary units. But the U.S.A. is not unique.

Groups with exactly the same kind of ideologies and sect mentality, and with exactly the same knowledge of how to make bombs, have existed in Sweden since the end of the 1980s.

Hate groups

The Swedish legal system does not forbid the organization of groups based on hatred. In one respect, in fact, the law is even more liberal than that of the U.S.A.: in Sweden it is more or less impossible to prosecute a neo-Nazi for either political terrorism or crimes against the constitution.

A Swedish racist who throws a bomb into a refugee camp—an act that would automatically attract a sentence of ten years' imprisonment in Italy—could possibly be sentenced to a few months in prison for arson. In Sweden the concept of "political terrorist" is reserved exclusively for foreigners, and only Kurds have ever been subjected to community detention for this offence.[2]

Since the late 1980s Swedish neo-Nazis have been setting up a political tendency under the name "Storms Nätverk" (Network Storm). The name derives from the journal *Storm*, which was published 1990–93, and since then has been succeeded by similar magazines such as *Blod och Ära* (Blood and Honor), *Gryning* (Dawn), *Nordland* (Northland) and *Valhall* (Valhalla).[3]

Terrorist groups

In substance, the journal *Storm* and its successors promulgate the ideology that the Aryan Nations and the American terrorist group the Order stand for. Most of the articles in *Storm* can be described as primitive hate propaganda aimed at Jews and immigrants. The basic tone is enthusiasm for terrorism and the romanticization of violence. Even worse, imprisoned members of the Order—"prisoners of war," according to the terminology used by *Storm*—are regular contributors of articles to the journal. One such writer is Alan Berg's murderer, David Lane.

In other words, foreign terrorists who have been given several life sentences send advice and instructions as to how Swedish race warriors should go about their business.

Network Storm is not a big movement. Like all terrorist groups it has a hard-core minority of about 150 people, and a few hundred more peripheral adherents. The makeup of the representative activists is more or less the same as in the U.S.A.—a mixture of traditional Nazis, skinheads, weapons freaks and out-and-out criminal elements.

In 1991 some of the enthusiasts formed Vitt Ariskt Motstånd (V.A.M.—White Aryan Resistance),[4] supposedly as an underground liberation army—a Swedish equivalent of the Order. As in the U.S.A., the underground warfare did not go particularly well. Let us just say that V.A.M. activists are not excessively talented.

Today Network Storm consists of ten or so militant neo-Nazi groups, of which the biggest is Riksfronten (R.F.—the National Front).[5] Among the other groups are Kreativistens Kyrka (the Church of the Creator),[6] Nationalsocialisterna (N.S.—the National Socialists) in Gothenburg,[7] and the prison organization Thuleringen (the Thule Circle).[8] The network is not strong enough to be a serious threat to our democratic system, but like all terrorist groups it can stir up a lot of mischief from time to time.

Should we take the threat of V.A.M. and similar organizations seriously when they claim that they intend to start an armed underground war aimed at the Swedish "Z.O.G. regime"? The only way to answer that question is to take a closer look at what they actually do.

Since the early '90s several activists have been charged and convicted of various crimes. Storm members have broken into Lidingö police station and stolen pistols. Some activists have broken into military arms depots or been convicted for having stolen weapons from various military camps. Others have been convicted of serious crimes, including bank robbery, while still more have been convicted of grievous bodily harm, attempted murder and at least seven cases of actual murder.

In total the Network Storm hard core have already been found guilty of political crimes on such a scale that in many countries they would have been banned as a terrorist organization, and their leaders locked up in maximum-security prisons.

Without attempting to predict specific events, one can nevertheless anticipate one outcome: sooner or later an Oklahoma massacre will take place in Sweden as well. All the ingredients are already in place: hatred, fanaticism, a sect mentality and a romanticization of violence.

With hindsight we shall conclude—just as they have now done in the U.S.A.—that when a political sect maintains, year out and year in, that it is going to launch an armed attack on the government of the day, it is inevitable that sooner or later some of its members will do something very, very silly.

Notes

1. The attack took place on April 19, 1995.
2. The Kurds are one of the largest immigrant groups in Sweden. Some came to Sweden from Turkey, having been members of the P.K.K. guerrilla movement. When Swedish Prime Minister Olof Palme was assassinated in 1986, the police directed their suspicions at the organization, their theory being that the murder was in revenge for the Swedish security police's monitoring of several P.K.K. supporters. The investigation found no evidence that the P.K.K. was involved in the murder, but nevertheless led to the Kurdish population being singled out, and subsequently feeling persecuted.
3. The magazines *Blod och Ära, Gryning* and *Valhall* were in the first half of the 1990s among the leading right-wing newspapers in Sweden. Their content was focused upon explicit racism and hatred of democracy.
4. White Aryan Resistance was a Nazi network that declared war against the Swedish state. The group was inspired by U.S. terror-oriented Nazism and was responsible for a series of crimes, among others the robbing of a bank and the theft of weapons from a police station.
5. The National Front was a fascist organization formed in 1991 as a continuation of the Swedish Association of the Future, but was disbanded only a few years after its inception. The organization's first leader was sent to prison for aggravated assault.
6. The Church of the Creator was a Swedish branch of the U.S. organization of the same name. The Swedish division, led by Tommy Rydén, was formed in 1989 with an ideology built on Nazi ideas, anti-Semitism, race biology and the leadership principle.
7. N.S. Gothenburg was a local Nazi group in Sweden's second largest city. The group was active during the first half of the 1990s and became known for organizing several concerts with international white-power bands.
8. The Thule Circle was an organization for imprisoned Nazis founded in 1993 by people linked to the Nazi network White Aryan Resistance.

THE NEW POPULAR MOVEMENT

Expo/Svartvitt, no. 3/4—1999

The three bomb attacks in London in spring[1] attracted attention from over the whole world. Nail bombs were used, intended to cause maximum injuries. The targets were immigrant enclaves and a gay bar. When 23-year-old David Copeland was arrested after an intensive police investigation, terrorism acquired a face. The police were quick to announce that Copeland was "a one-off madman" with no political affiliations, and London heaved a collective sigh of relief.

The problem is that Scotland Yard was wrong.

For several years David Copeland had been active in various far-right contexts. He was a member of the neo-Nazi organization the British National Party (B.N.P.), and was one of the inner circle surrounding party leader John Tyndall. This is the Tyndall who, as early as the 1960s, was condemned as an activist in the neo-Nazi group Spearhead after a series of attacks on synagogues.

Authorities have a tendency to dismiss right-wing terrorists as "one-off madmen." This applies in England as much as it does in Sweden. There seems to be an inbuilt resistance to the thought that neo-Nazis are serious when they claim to want to demolish democratic society. There is a simple explanation for this: a "one-off madman" is less disturbing and easier to explain than the possibility that neo-Nazis are in fact organizing terrorist activities on an international scale.

Nevertheless, that seems to be the reality. The distance between Sweden and abroad is not considerable. The groups that organize terrorist activities in the U.S.A. and England have their henchmen in Sweden.

From a historical point of view, Nazism has always used terrorism as a battle strategy. In the postwar years the far right comprised isolated small sects that fought hard to tone down the more violent rhetoric.

For obvious reasons, postwar terrorism has been low-key and at times barely discernible. What has made it worth the effort of scraping below the surface has been its links to organized violence.

The strategy of tension

Terrorism got into its stride again with a series of bloody atrocities in Italy during the 1960s. The first large-scale attack was the Milan massacre in 1969, when about twenty people were killed by a bomb in a farmers' bank. The series of outrages culminated in the 1980 bombing of the railway station in Bologna, when almost a hundred people died.

The Italian terrorism was based on a so-called "strategy of tension," a theory launched by the fascist cell Ordine Nuovo (the New Order). By means of random, anonymous terror attacks Ordine Nuovo tried to create a state of chaos in Italy that would lead to a coup d'état. Fascist agitators infiltrated left-wing groups or created their own "anarchist battalions" that accepted responsibility for what had happened. Internal documents from the beginning of the 1980s define their aims:

> The first of our measures must be to create chaos in the state system [and] destroy the government's power structures. [...] We must take action via the courts and the Church in order to influence public opinion and demonstrate the shortcomings and incompetence of legal power processes. This will present us as the only possibility for establishing a social and political solution to the problem.

Italian terrorism very nearly achieved its aims. Several hundred people were killed in terrorist outrages, and at least one attempt at a coup d'état took place in 1970.

Political soldiers

After the Bologna massacre of 1980, a witch-hunt for terrorists was launched in Italy. One group of fascists from the so-called National Revolutionary Avant-Garde, led by Roberto Fiore, chose to go underground and fled the country. A few years later Fiore and his gang turned up in England, where they were assisted by the secretive neo-Nazi group the League of St. George.

The twenty or so activists eventually landed up in an English court, which rejected an Italian request for extradition. Fiore and his chums later became "advisers" to the British National Front.

The Italians were less than impressed by their namby-pamby and amateurish English colleagues, but took it upon themselves to introduce new revolutionary theories. A few of the younger National Front leaders paid diligent attention. One of them was Derek Holland, who wrote a pamphlet in the mid-1980s entitled "The Political Soldier." It was translated into Swedish by Bevara Sverige Svenskt (B.S.S.—Keep Sweden Swedish), the precursor of the Sweden Democrats. Holland's pamphlet, which is still sold by most similar groups, demands that members of the movement must be trained to become dedicated "soldiers," rather than normal activists.

The Turner Diaries

In the mid-1980s European militants began to be influenced by the American far right, which produced dozens of handbooks on "the theory and practice of race war." Their "Bible" is the book *The Turner Diaries*, written at the end of the 1970s by William Pierce, the leader of the neo-Nazi organization the National Alliance.

Hatred of the Jews and conspiracy theories

Theories of terrorism have developed step by step over the last twenty years. In Italy the concept of "the third position" came into being—neither capitalism nor communism, but fascism. The Italian fascists were more interested in questions of power and the state than in traditional race biology. When the ideas achieved a foothold in northern Europe by way of the National Front in England, racism began to play a more prominent role. The Americans contributed by formulating hatred of the Jews and anti-Semitic conspiracy theories.

The Turner Diaries claims that Jewish agents secretly control centers of power in the Western world. The government—irrespective of whether it is Bill Clinton in the U.S.A. or Göran Persson in Sweden—is called Z.O.G., an abbreviation for "Zionist Occupation Government," which "works in secret to destroy the white Aryan race." The militant groups maintain that the only way to fight Z.O.G. is to declare RAHOWA, an abbreviation for "Racial Holy War."

A result of this development is a change in the targets attacked by terrorists. The main enemy is no longer individual immigrants or even individual Jews, but democracy itself and the government institutions in the U.S.A. and Western Europe. That is why a federal building in Oklahoma City is a target for bombers, and why Swedish neo-Nazis are urged to shoot police officers.[2]

Racial Holy War

At the beginning of the 1980s an underground fighting unit was formed in the U.S.A. called the Order, whose aim was to start a race war.

At the beginning of the 1990s the group acquired a Swedish offshoot in the form of Vitt Ariskt Motstånd (V.A.M.—White

Aryan Resistance), which, like their American colleagues, plundered weapons depots and raided banks to finance their "holy race war."

Leaderless resistance

Both the Order in the U.S.A. and V.A.M. in Sweden failed. A number of activists were arrested and imprisoned—in the U.S.A. for between forty and ninety years, in Sweden for a few months or a couple of years.

The militant organizations drew certain conclusions. There was nothing wrong with the aim of "annihilating Z.O.G.," but the state—that is the power of the police—was too strong to be challenged in open guerrilla warfare.

The next armchair revolutionary to come to grips with the task of pointing terrorism in a new direction was Louis Beam, one of the leaders of the racist organization the Ku Klux Klan. Beam formulated a concept he called "leaderless resistance."

Beam advocates a sort of spontaneous terrorism carried out by "dedicated and convinced political soldiers." Terrorism can comprise all kinds of violent action—the bombing of law courts and police stations, letter bombs sent to politicians, the murder of "race traitors." The latter category obviously includes the journalists Peter Karlsson and Katarina Larsson.[3]

The advantage of "leaderless resistance," according to its advocates, is that the terrorism is not organized by a specific group and does not have formal leaders. As a result, Z.O.G.'s agents—the police—have difficulty in identifying and catching the perpetrators. Terrorism becomes an anonymous action, something of a "popular movement," which "creates fear in society."

The laserman as a model

One of the people frequently held up as a model for "leaderless resistance" is the laserman, John Ausonius, who shot ten immigrants and killed one in the course of his rampages in the early 1990s.

It should be pointed out that virtually all the notorious "one-off madmen" such as Buford Furrow and his like in the U.S.A., who have indulged in murder orgies this past year, are associated with groups that preach the gospel of "leaderless resistance."

Sweden too has its terrorist philosophers. When the militant organization gave up its V.A.M. concept in 1993, the question of how the struggle would be financed remained. Bank robbery was no longer a possibility—at least, not as the main source of income. The police were too skillful at solving puzzles and too many race crusaders became "political prisoners."

When white-power music made its breakthrough in 1993, the financial problems were solved. The sales of C.D.s became a lucrative source of income and several of the groups preaching militant struggle reinvented themselves as production companies. The most important of these, the organization based on V.A.M. and the journal *Storm*, became *Nordland*, with four-colour printing and sophisticated layouts.

Another company is Ragnarock Records in Helsingborg, one of the biggest producers of white-power music

and hate propaganda in Europe. Ragnarock Records is
in fact the collective name for about ten or so different
enterprises that sell everything from video films to Hitler monographs, terrorist manuals and survivalist knives.
The political organization behind Ragnarock is Blood and
Honour/Scandinavia and Combat 18 International.

Blood and Honour

Blood and Honour was formed originally as a rallying point
for the skinhead movement in England in the 1980s, but it
was taken over by the terrorist organization Combat 18; the
figures stand for the letters A.H., in other words, Adolf Hitler.

C18 preached a combination of organized terrorism and
"leaderless resistance." It was at its strongest in the mid-
1990s, but more recently has had major problems with the
British authorities. The former C18 leader Charlie Sargent
was sentenced to life imprisonment for murder, and the
organization is now led by Will Browning, who advocates
bombing campaigns throughout Europe.

Over the years C18 activists have conducted violent
attacks on both anti-racists and opponents within the neo-
Nazi movement. The organization is behind several of the
last few years' bombing campaigns.[4]

As the British police have put increasing pressure on
C18, the organization has shrunk and nowadays boasts
barely twenty members in London. But the fact that there
are so few of them has not been a worry for the C18 leaders.
For some years now they have been busy moving all their
activities abroad, notably to Ragnarock Records in Helsingborg and to the video enterprise NS88 in Denmark.

Ragnarock—or rather Blood and Honour/Scandinavia—has thus become the political and organizational center for the most violent neo-Nazi tendencies in Europe.

"Blue pigs"

There is very little cause for doubt about the policies advocated by Blood and Honour in Scandinavia. In its pamphlets, in speeches given at its meetings and on its Internet home-page, the organization urges "leaderless resistance" and a violent struggle against democracy.

In June this year, a few days before the car bomb atrocities in Nacka and Malmö, the police in Denmark raided a house on the island of Langeland which had served as a secret meeting place for Blood & Honour. Several people were arrested, and one of the leaders, Erik Blücher, condemned the raid as a typical state overreaction.

There were more outspoken comments on the Blood & Honour home page. The main enemies were accused under the heading "Red scum and blue pigs": the anti-racist demonstrators who had turned up on Langeland, and the police—"the pigs in blue"—who had taken part in the raid on the building. Blood and Honour have no hesitation in making blatant threats aimed at police officers who take action against their organization. The attack on the building on Langeland is described as follows: "Z.O.G.'s blue mafia pounced. The attacks were pure harassment spiced with a dose of terror. Ruben, the lead singer [in the Swedish band Hets mot Folkgrupp (Racial Agitation)], was seriously injured, but we managed to take a photograph of the pig in blue, and one of these days I hope that Aryan justice will be done."

The double murder of two police officers in Malexander is hailed thus: "The gun battle between National Socialists who liberated bank funds and the Z.O.G. troops is just revenge for the murder of Mikael Krusell by the police in Malmö in 1991."[5] A week or so later the scene of the murder in Malexander was vandalized and swastikas sprayed on every available surface.

Blood and Honour also commented on the car bomb attack that killed Peter Karlsson and Katarina Larsson in Nacka: "The bombing of the journalist Peter Karlsson was [...] a totally justified action in self-defence . . ."

Notes

1. On three successive weekends in April 1999, nail bombs were detonated in Brixton, Brick Lane and Soho.
2. In 1999, two Swedish police officers were murdered outside the small village of Malexander following a bank robbery. After having chased the robbers by car, the police officers were stopped on the road and brutally executed. All three robbers had a background in the Swedish Nazi movement and were attempting to raise money for their new right-wing organization. One of the robbers ultimately confessed that he had murdered the policemen alone. The Malexander murders is one of the most famous cases in Swedish criminal history.
3. In the 1990s journalists Peter Karlsson and Katarina Larsson wrote several major scoops about the Swedish white-power movement. In 1999, Peter Karlsson and his son were victims of a car-bomb attack. Both survived. The police never made any arrests, but suspicion was directed at the white-power movement that the couple had been reporting about.
4. The English Nazi group Combat 18 was formed in 1992 and became known as an extremely violent and brutal organization. In 1999 it was suspected of having carried out a series of bomb attacks in London. It later turned out that a lone assailant who

had perpetrated the attacks. He sympathized with the extreme right but was not active in the C18.

5. On November 29, 1991, the 23-year-old skinhead Mikael Krusell was shot dead by a policeman in Lund outside Malmö. Krusell had been in Lund to participate in a right-wing demonstration. The policeman was never brought to justice, and Mikael Krusell has since become one of the Nazi movement's martyrs.

DEMOCRACY IN EUROPE?

Expo no. 2—2003

In 1997 *Expo* made a study of the far right in Europe, country by country. The result was most interesting.

In twenty-five out of thirty-seven countries, far right or extreme nationalist groups were represented in parliament. In six of the former Eastern bloc countries the far right exerted influence on the government. In most European countries there were well-organized, militant extra-parliamentary movements. In nine countries, not least in the former Yugoslavia, there were more or less active terrorist groups.

When the distribution of votes in various countries was analyzed, it turned out that in several densely populated countries the extreme right was just as strong as, or even stronger than had been the case in the last free elections of the 1930s before the fascist dictatorships came to power.

All comparisons of that nature are of course questionable; the situation in the 1930s cannot be compared with the situation seventy years later.

Nevertheless the existence of active anti-democratic groups gives an indication of the state that democracy finds itself in. The common denominator for all these parties is a calling into question of the legitimacy of democratic society. The most common propaganda message is the claim that somehow or other democratic politicians are scoundrels who cheat and line their pockets at the expense of ordinary people, and who have "sold out" or "betrayed" their country.

There is no doubt that extreme nationalistic thinking has expanded dramatically over the past twenty years. Groups that as late as the 1970s hid away in cellars and received only a very small percentage of the votes in general elections are now mass movements supported by millions of voters. A dramatic political sea change has taken place.

Democratic politicians have had big problems when it comes to pinning down and refuting the new extreme right. Unlike the activists of the 1930s, their modern counterparts do not wear black uniforms, but immaculately tailored Armani suits. They saunter into the European parliament and national governments with winning smiles and assurances that they are members of "democratic" parties through and through.

Politicians who try to tone down the significance of the growth of these groups like to proclaim that the parliamentary far right is "adapting" to the democratic system—and thereby becoming harmless and ineffective.

However, the reality is that just as often the democratic parties adapt to the rhetoric and propaganda of the far right. An example of this is the way the policies of the Danish government have changed since the Dansk Folkeparti (D.F.—Danish People's Party) held the balance of power in parliament. At a stroke, views that ten years ago would have been condemned as crude racism and xenophobia have become acceptable. Pia Kjaersgaard succeeded in setting the tone for the general election's rhetoric with crude populist rants and hate propaganda aimed at Muslims.

An example of parties poised between extremism and respectability is the French Mouvement pour la France (M.P.F.), led by the aristocrat Philippe de Villiers. The party is classed as "national liberal"—an interesting new label—and pursues policies that seem to advocate the total isolation of France from the rest of the world. Among the party's members of the European Parliament are respectable business leaders, academics and former Gaullists.

The party could have been an ultra-conservative but nevertheless respectable party had there not been the continually recurring "but"—that democracy in their eyes is something that applies only to Europeans.

The M.P.F.'s immigration policies include a series of proposals that would make it "unattractive" for immigrants to reside in Europe. The party is a fanatical opponent of the E.U. but wants to establish a pan-European database to register and possibly expel all forms of "illegal immigration." It is not clear how "illegal" is to be defined, but a series of new special regulations would separate the wheat from the chaff. Mosques would be built only if members agree in writing, legally binding, to "obey the laws of France"—as if there had been any question of this not being the case otherwise.

Today it is no longer a question of small Mickey Mouse parties supported by 1.5 percent of the electorate hiding away in cellars. It is a matter of millions of voters aligning themselves with a movement whose aims have not changed noticeably since the 1930s. These parties present a challenge to our democratic and open society. They will be on the agenda for the foreseeable future.

LIVING WITH PIA KJAERSGAARD

Expo no. 1-2—2002

Before September 11 last year, racism and anti-immigration attitudes were not an electoral issue in Denmark. Hardly any other party paid any attention to the views of Pia Kjaersgaard and the Dansk Folkeparti (D.F.—Danish People's Party). But in November Kjaersgaard won just over 12 percent of the votes cast, and held the balance of power when it came to forming a new government. Life in Denmark had changed overnight, and it is always being held up as a model by the Sverigedemokrater (S.D.—Sweden Democrats).

"The real winner of the election was the Danish mass media," says Bashy Quraishy.

Bashy Quraishy was born in India, grew up in Pakistan and was educated in the U.S.A., Germany and England. He now lives in Copenhagen, and is active as the chairman of E.N.A.R., the European Network Against Racism, which organizes rather more than six hundred non-state anti-racist groups. It is one of Europe's biggest grass-roots movements.

During the spring of 2002 Bashy Quraishy visited Stockholm on two occasions to deliver a lecture—first in February at a seminar arranged jointly by *Expo*, the Swedish Helsinki Committee and the Human Rights Fund, and then at a seminar arranged by Integrationsverket (the Integration Office) on March 21, International Day for the Elimination of Racial Discrimination. Both lectures concentrated mainly on the Denmark that emerged in the wake of the D.F.'s election success. Bashy's criticism of the Danish mass media is unsparing:

"Before September 11, our newspapers were fairly normal products of a normal Scandinavian country. But after the attack on the World Trade Center floodgates were opened in ways that nobody would have thought possible. It suddenly became legitimate to harass Muslims in general and Arabs in particular.

"Newspaper placards for perfectly normal daily newspapers suddenly began to look like propaganda posters for the National Front. On a daily basis Muslims were described as 'a threat to Denmark' and to Danish welfare. Muslims were threatening to introduce sharia law. Muslims were threatening to inundate Den-mark if nobody closed the floodgates. Immigrants were accused of gang rape, criminality, terrorism, religious fanaticism and hatred of Denmark.

"Not even if Pia Kjaersgaard had been given a free hand to control the Danish press could she have imagined in her wildest dreams that, of their own accord, the mass media would have promulgated the most unpleasantly racist parts of the Danish People's Party's program. And the propaganda continued for weeks on end."

Bashy Quraishy believes that as a result, Pia Kjaersgaard's electoral breakthrough was hardly a surprise. Seldom have political developments played into the hands of a racist party as effectively as in Denmark in the autumn of 2001.

Hopes invested in the Kjaersgaard effect

Denmark and the success of the Danish People's Party have quickly become an example for Swedish nationalists to follow. The party naturally hopes that the Kjaersgaard effect will sneak over the Sound and at least as far as Skåne, which is the home province of the S.D.'s leading light, Sten Andersson.

The Sweden Democrats seldom miss an opportunity to thump out the message that "democracy rules in Denmark." This is an indication of how the party defines democracy.

"In fact," Bashy Quraishy maintains, "the successes registered by the Danish People's Party are the green light for the biggest dismantling of the democratic system that has ever taken place in a Western European country.

"The Danish government, a coalition between the liberal Venstre (Left) party and the Konservativt Folkepatti (Conservative People's Party), is being held hostage by the Danish People's Party. In order to remain in power, the government has to adjust its policies to appease Pia

Kjaersgaard and satisfy a series of demands made by her party. It is a catastrophic development, but what is most surprising is how incredibly quickly such moods of hatred can be whipped up."

The prime minister is "a traitor"

Developments in Denmark over the last six months have also led to clashes between the Swedish and Danish governments, which led to a war of words that has drawn widespread comment. Swedish politicians such as Mona Sahlin and others have been caustically critical, while the Sweden Democrats, not unexpectedly, have supported the Danish People's Party.

Swedish politicians who criticize the Danish resolutions have been described as "anti-democrats" and "traitors"— exactly the same terms used by the Danish People's Party in crude diatribes during the election campaign. Far-right propaganda often includes emotional but irrelevant personal attacks.

A poster produced by the Danish People's Party's youth section depicted former prime minister Poul Nyrup Rasmussen naked from the waist up on the lap of a veiled Arab woman. The headline was: "Seduced by the Enemy—an important election, a cynical woman, a man under pressure in a dangerous alliance."

All the time the Danish People's Party spread hate-propaganda about how democratic politicians were "selling out Denmark" to a foreign occupying power—immigrants.

The present Danish government under Prime Minister Anders Fogh Rasmussen ignores or attempts to circumvent binding international agreements on human rights. The horrific aspect of this is that democracy is being used as an excuse—Rasmussen maintains that processes "have observed the rules" and that "the people are having their say." The government has come up with a number of proposals to change laws and make them more anti-pathetic to immigrants, formulated by the Danish People's Party, which—if they are passed and become law—risk creating real ethnic unrest in Denmark in the long run.

Human rights institutions are being abolished

Here are some of the proposals the Sweden Democrats are enthusiastic about:

The right of immigrant families to be reunited will be abolished.

The possibility of being reunited with parents over the age of sixty will be repealed.

The possibility of an immigrant to obtain Danish citizenship will be made significantly more difficult.

Foreigners cannot obtain a permanent residential visa until they have been in Denmark for seven years.

Greatly reduced wages during the first year of work in order to dissuade foreigners from seeking employment.

The loss of a temporary residence permit if a foreigner applies for normal social benefits.

Immigrants who wish to marry a foreign citizen may not
do so below the age of twenty-four.

If the marriage lasts for fewer than seven years, the foreign party is forced to leave Denmark.

In addition to the above changes in the law, a whole battery of minor measures is being proposed with the aim of
reducing immigrants' welfare rights, legal status and opportunities of living active lives in Denmark. These include the
abolishing of the right to home-language tuition, an over-
haul of the grants system for ethnic free schools, a require-
ment that Christianity should be reintroduced as a main
subject, and so on.

A serious curtailment of the traditional democratic system is that the Danish government has announced big reduc-
tions in grants to both government and non-government
organizations dedicated to matters of human rights.

The organizations most immediately affected are the
Ethnic Equality Agency, which is the only state organization working to combat ethnic discrimination in Denmark, and the Danish Centre for Human Rights, whose
chairman, Morten Kjaerum, has been forced to resign. The
Centre for Human Rights has attracted huge international
respect for its research.

"All these are steps in the wrong direction, steps away
from ideals of integration and a society based on solidarity," Bashy Quraishy argues. "Today the victims are ethnic
minorities; tomorrow the discrimination might just as well
affect the homeless, single parents, pensioners or some
other group that is suddenly regarded as being a millstone

round the neck of society, and becomes the object of hate campaigns.

"One effect is that a lot of grass-roots organizations and associations for ethnic minorities lose large amounts of their financial backing. The highly regarded Danish Refugee Council—the only independent institution supporting victims of racial discrimination—has already sacked some of its employees after receiving advance notice from the government of the withdrawal of regular grants."

Apartheid in the labor market

Bashy Quraishy maintains that one of the most controversial aspects of the proposed measures is the suggestion that immigrants with temporary residence visas should receive a kick-start on the labor market by being forced to accept comparatively lower wages—up to 50 percent lower has been mentioned—during the first year of employment. The proposal is presented as "an integration-friendly way of introducing immigrants into working life."

"This is obviously a proposal that no serious trade union will ever accept," Quraishy says. "It implies a society that intentionally builds in salary differences based on ethnicity. There are special words for this sort of system. One of the commonest is apartheid.

"It also means that Denmark guarantees that, for the foreseeable future, people with foreign backgrounds will be worse off and have lower living standards than native Danes. And it means in turn that immigrants will be forced into the black market or into the criminal economy.

"And of course, if ethnic minorities are forced to accept significantly lower wages, they will be exploited by unscrupulous firms. We don't need a degree in political science to know that the whole system is tailor-made to produce real differences based on ethnicity between Danes and immigrant workers."

Too much for Haider to stomach

The Danish neo-racism—which the Sweden Democrats welcome as a model for Sweden—has attracted a lot of attention abroad.

Mary Robinson, the U.N. Commissioner for Human Rights, is so worried that she has alerted the international community and urged them to keep an eye on developments in Denmark.

The leaders of the Nordic liberal parties have sent a joint letter to their Danish party colleague, Prime Minister Fogh Rasmussen, spelling out detailed criticism of the anti-foreigner politics being adopted by his government.

"We find ourselves in the absurd position of discovering that the measures proposed by the Danish government are so off-putting that even Jörg Haider cannot stomach them and wants to distance himself from Denmark. When Pia Kjaersgaard recently visited Vienna, Haider refused to meet her."

How should Sweden react?

"As far as E.N.A.R. is concerned, we think that in spite of everything the Danish government is sensitive to international criticism. Sweden has a well-deserved international reputation for standing up for human rights and against injustice.

"When I delivered a lecture in Sweden I asked the Swedish government not to suppress criticism, but to be bold and discuss Danish racism in the E.U. and in other international contexts. I'm very pleased to be able to confirm that several Swedish politicians, not least Mona Sahlin,[1] have done just that.

"She and other politicians will no doubt be subjected to furious outbursts from Kjaersgaard, but the most dangerous thing that can happen just now is that the 'Danish effect' could spill over into other Scandinavian countries— that there could be a domino effect with other democratic politicians singing from the same hymn sheet as Denmark."

Note

1. Mona Sahlin is one of the Swedish Social Democrats' best known politicians. She has long experience in political life and has previously held the posts of party leader and Minister for Gender Equality. Because of her strong commitment to gay rights and her fight against discrimination, she is the Swedish extreme right's main object of hate.

THE RETURN OF ANTI-SEMITISM

Expo/Monitor no. 3—1998

"What is a Jew doing when he looks at an ashtray?"—"Some genealogical research!" The "joke" is taken from ProPatria's home page on the Internet. It is one of about forty under the heading "Humour" and the sub-heading "Jew." There is a similar collection of racist jokes under the sub-heading "Negroes."

Fifteen years ago—and probably as recently as ten years ago—the publication of such obviously crude anti-Semitic propaganda would have been unthinkable. The legally responsible publisher would have been the subject of a police investigation, charged and found guilty. But that is now no longer the case.

Nevertheless it is not particularly difficult to track down a legally responsible publisher. When I asked the question, it took *Expo* Research no more than a couple of hours to establish that ProPatria's home page belongs to "Mats," previously resident in Solna. This is not the first time that "Mats" has appeared on the Internet in a neo-Nazi context. He used to be responsible for the Gjallarhorn ("Yelling Horn") home page, which has now closed down.

It is of course no surprise that neo-Nazis promulgate hatred of the Jews. After all, the keystone of classical Nazi ideology was anti-Semitism. But since the Second World War—after the Holocaust—hatred of Nazism was so widespread that there was simply no market for anti-Semitism.

This does not mean that the Nazi hatred of the Jews no longer applied; it was simply that it was no longer practical for neo-Nazi groups to admit to it if they wished to survive politically. Hatred of the Jews was thus removed from their official propaganda and kept to internal meetings. In the neo-Nazi press the word "Jew" was replaced by suitable code words such as "cosmopolitans," "internationalists" and—from the 1960s onward—"Zionists." Veteran Nazis and prominent ideologues who encouraged hatred of the Jews long before the war—the Swede Per Engdahl is an excellent example—changed their tune and denied that they had ever been anti-Semitic. To admit in public that you were anti-Semitic was to be branded as crazy.

But that is no longer the case today.

ProPatria's home page on the Internet is neither the only nor the worst of its kind. It is one of dozens. Today there are more openly anti-Semitic pages on the Internet than ever before. There is a steady stream of new ones appearing all the time. Not a single legally responsible publisher has been charged and found guilty of racist propaganda on the Internet.

This can mean only one thing: people who have been producing anti-Semitic hate propaganda in recent years have succeeded in stretching the tolerance limits of society in general. Anti-Semitic propaganda of a type that was unthinkable fifteen years ago is now so common that the police and prosecutors no longer find it worth their while to investigate it, and that the mass media and political organizations can no longer be bothered to follow it up.

ProPatria and similar propaganda groups have thus been awarded a remarkable special status—they are not responsible for criminal activities.

Anti-Semitic undercurrents

The fact that hatred of Jews was toned down after the war naturally does not mean that it disappeared from the ideological menu. Ever since 1945 anti-Semitism has lived on as a sort of insidious undercurrent, but only a few uncompromising Nazis—usually unknown madmen—have dared to air their anti-Semitism in public. From a political point of view they have been insignificant, but they played a role as upholders of a tradition.

One example from the 1950s was Einar Åberg, whose anti-Semitic leaflets and pamphlets attracted attention and condemnation from all over Europe.[1]

Einar Åberg also serves as an indicator that a sea change has taken place. Compared with the tidal wave of anti-Semitic manifestations with which Europe is currently awash in the form of white-power music, magazines, radio programs and video films, Åberg's lampoons seem almost harmless.

Another difference is that the political and cultural establishment in Europe no longer reacts as angrily to anti-Semitic propaganda as was the case with Einar Åberg. If, for example, Ahmed Rami had been broadcasting on Radio Islam in the 1950s, or if *Nordland* had published its notorious hate-filled attack on the Bonnier family at that time, leader writers in *Le Monde*, *The Times* and *Der Spiegel* would all have focused their attention on Sweden. Authors, lawyers and politicians would have sent petitions to the Swedish government, urging it to take measures against such neo-Nazi hate propaganda.

One reason for this lack of response from intellectuals is of course the fact that Jew-hating propagandists are no longer restricted to an occasional Einar Åberg, a Colin Jordan, a Francis Parker Yockey and a few dozen more notorious Nazis who could be dismissed as madmen. There are many more Jew-haters around today. Anti-Semitic propaganda is no longer restricted to occasional trickles from isolated pens. In more or less every European country, not least in the Scandinavian countries, there are nowadays several well-organized anti-Semitic hate groups with astonishingly large financial resources.

There is also a noticeable difference in the attitudes of the anti-Semites themselves. In the postwar years and until long into the 1980s, hatred of the Jews was something the neo-Nazi propagandists tried to distance themselves from.

Very few neo-Nazi leaders were openly anti-Semitic in their public pronouncements, and when the mass media turned their attention to any such group they soon withdrew into the shadows.

But today's anti-Semites from Ahmed Rami to *Nordland* and the National Socialist Front (N.S.F.) are not ashamed of their hatred of the Jews. On the contrary, they state confidently and proudly that "Hitler was right."

Revisionism as an icebreaker

Nazi historical revisionism is the branch of anti-Semitism that has paid most attention to the Jews since the war. Unlike the political activists, the revisionists have concentrated on appearing to be "objective" and "serious" researchers. Their main aim has not been to stir up anti-Semitism, but to exonerate Hitler and create mystery and doubt concerning the Holocaust, suggesting it never took place.

They have been successful in that respect. A lot of interest was attracted by the report from C.E.I.F.O. (the Centre for Research in International Migration and Ethic Relations at Stockholm University) on the attitude of young people to democracy and racism, published last year. It showed that as many as 17 percent of Swedish young people are not convinced that the Holocaust actually took place.

There are no corresponding statistics from earlier years, but it would have been very interesting to compare those figures with the results of similar research in the 1970s, for instance. At a guess—and it is pure speculation—the number of young people who doubted the existence of the Holocaust would have been virtually zero.

The two people who have done most to establish neo-Nazi historical revisionism in Scandinavia are Ditlieb Felderer and Ahmed Rami, closely followed by Alfred Olsen in Norway.[2]

What is interesting about this trio is the way in which they have all broken with the traditional attitudes of international revisionists. Unlike Robert Faurisson,[3] for instance, who has tried hard to dissociate himself from anti-Semitism, Felderer, Rami and Olsen have never tried to hide the fact that what motivates them above all else is their hatred of the Jews.

When Rami was prosecuted at the beginning of the 1990s for inciting racial hatred in his Radio Islam broadcasts, most of the neo-Nazi movement remained silent. They only began to congratulate him after he was released from prison in 1992. Tommy Rydén, then leader of the Kreativistens Kyrka (Church of the Creator), spoke on Radio Islam, and in 1993 members of Riksfronten (the National Front) acted as bodyguards for Rami during a visit by Robert Faurisson. In 1996 *Nordland* published a long interview with Rami.

In many respects Rami has acted as a pioneer for the neo-Nazi movement. He succeeded in breaking the taboo against anti-Semitic propaganda which the movement had not dared to express so openly for many years.

A tidal wave of anti-Semitism

A random scan of neo-Nazi magazines from the 1970s shows that the word "Jew" rarely if ever appears. There are occasional references to "cosmopolitans" or "Zionists," but open anti-Semitic propaganda seldom appears in their columns.

Nowadays, however, anti-Semitism is the most important ideological element in almost any neo-Nazi journal
you care to name. This phenomenon is not unique to Scandinavia, but is a trend throughout most of Europe.

It could be said that the ideological focus of neo-Nazism
on the Jews began in Sweden at the end of the 1980s. A magazine that took up the cudgels for the new anti-Semitism
was *Vit Rebell* (White Rebel), published by Peter Melander
and Göran Gustavsson in Södertälje. *Vit Rebell* was eventually replaced by the journal *Storm*, which was for a while
the mouthpiece of Vitt Ariskt Motstånd (V.A.M.—White
Aryan Resistance). *Storm* itself was later transformed into
Nordland, now one of the leading players in attempts to
breathe new life into classical anti-Semitism.

Nordland and the National Socialist Front are the two
most important sources of undisguised hatred of Jews in
Sweden. Last year on November 8, just before the Kristall-
nacht memorial events in Stockholm, the N.S.F. organized the first specifically anti-Jewish demonstration in
Sweden since the Second World War. The slogans were
unmistakable: "Crush the power of the Jews" and "Crush
democracy."

Twenty years ago, and probably as recently as five or
six years ago, the N.S.F. demonstration would have been
unthinkable. But today it scarcely raises an eyebrow. The
Jews are back as "enemy number one."

Spreading throughout society

In the 1920s and 1930s anti-Semitism was part of the European cultural heritage. For many people who would never

have dreamed of calling themselves National Socialists it was natural to regard the Jews with suspicion and hostility.

In that respect anti-Semitism had become an integral part of the European cultural heritage. That is why it was not unusual for ordinary novels from the 1920s, and even novels politically hostile to Nazism, to depict Jews in more or less the same stereotypical way as the Nazis described them.

This cultural anti-Semitism was an important reason why Nazi anti-Semitism became so widespread, and there is now a danger that anti-Semitism could once more become common even outside neo-Nazi circles.

It is not surprising that dogmatic anti-Semitism is preached by an Ahmed Rami or by groups such as *Nordland* or the National Socialist Front. Nor is it surprising that activists within those groups promulgate hatred of the Jews on home pages on the Internet.

But this last year has seen a tendency for anti-Semitism to start spreading outside the ranks of militant neo-Nazism. First in the queue are a number of "respectable racists" in populist and anti-immigrant circles. Typical of several of these groups is that they claim respectability within the mainstream, and try to project themselves as "anti-racist patriots" or "reasonable nationalists."

Obviously these groups have suddenly performed a 180-degree turn overnight and now appear openly as anti-Semites. Most of the "respectable" activists would rather die than be exposed as anti-Semitic propagandists. Nevertheless it is obvious that they cannot steer clear of the propaganda spread by the neo-Nazi groups—which is hardly surprising, since activists from the borderland between populism and neo-Nazism have thus far been their only real support group. Their propaganda is significantly more stealthy and insidious. Let me give a few examples.

The racist lobby group Fri Information, whose leader is the former Swedish Conservative Party M.P. Eva Bergqvist, has a home page on the Internet with links to various obscure groups. One of the links is to Glistrup's home page in Denmark, which contains revisionist and anti-Semitic material of the crudest kind.[4]

Another example is the closely related group Blågula frågor (B.G.F., "Blue and Yellow Questions"), which is run by Jan Milld and Anders Sundholm.[5] Among the many topics taken up by B.G.F. in recent times is the Holocaust. The group recently published a vicious attack on Stéphane Bruchfeld, the author of a book on the Holocaust of which the government purchased multiple copies for educational use. B.G.F. makes no attempt to argue against the content of the book, but instead produced a long article casting doubt on Bruchfeld's scholarship and legitimacy as a researcher.[6]

The homepage Exponering (Exposure), which is closely allied to B.G.F., has recently moved after it was discovered that the page was based in the web hotel provided by the neo-Nazi group Alt.media. Exponering has links to Hvit Ungdom (White Youth) in Norway, and similar organizations.

Many more examples could be given, but the inevitable conclusion is that attitudes to anti-Semitism are becoming lax in the populistic far right.

How quickly the trend spreads remains to be seen. But the question is how long it will be before the first member of an established political party stands up in parliament and demands that "the power of the Jews" in Sweden be curtailed.

Notes

1. Einar Åberg was active in several Swedish National Socialist organizations during the Second World War. After the war he continued to spread anti-Semitic propaganda both in Sweden and abroad. His extensive distribution aroused anger throughout the world and in 1948, with the help of international pressure, Sweden introduced its law on incitement to racial hatred, initially known as Lex Åberg. Einar Åberg was convicted several times for spreading anti-Semitism, only ceasing to be active in the mid-1960s due to illness.

2. Felderer, Rami and Olsen are some of Scandinavia's most influential Holocaust deniers. Ditlieb Felderer was born in Austria in 1942 and came to Sweden as a child. In the 1970s he began to translate Holocaust denial literature, and has since become renowned for having questioned the authenticity of Anne Frank's diary. Ahmed Rami came to Sweden from Morocco in 1973 as a refugee. In the 1980s he ran the anti-Semitic radio program, Radio Islam. In 1990 he was sentenced for incitement to racial hatred. Today, Radio Islam has one of the world's most comprehensive anti-Semitic websites. The Norwegian Alfred Olsen led the ultra-Catholic anti-Semitic one-man organization People's Resistance and is a fervent Holocaust denier.

3. The French academic Robert Faurisson is one of the world's best known Holocaust deniers. As early as the 1970s he claimed that there had never been a genocide against Jews during the Second World War. Since then he has repeatedly been condemned for his theories about the Holocaust.

4. Mogens Glistrup is a Danish politician who became known in the 1970s for refusing to pay taxes to the Danish state. In 1972 he founded the populist Progress Party, which quickly grew in popularity. By the 1980s the party had become increasingly xenophobic. Glistrup was expelled from the party in 1990 and

was welcomed back ten years later, but by then the party had lost its appeal. Glistrup laid the foundations for the xenophobic populism that has been a major ingredient in the rhetoric of several subsequent right-wing populist parties.

5. The magazine *Blågula frågor* was first published in 1994. Its xenophobic agenda was exemplified by its frequent criticism of the Swedish migration policy.

6. Stéphane Bruchfeld is one of Sweden's leading historians on the Holocaust, based at the University of Uppsala. He is, among other things, co-author of the book *Tell Ye Your Children—A Book about the Holocaust in Europe 1933–1945* (Regeringskansliet Levande Historia, 1998).

THE WORLD PICTURE
OF SUPERSTITION

Internationalen no. 39—1983

"Astrology (fr. *Greek* astér, *star*, and logos, *speech*)—
the art of foreseeing the future from the stars. A. has a
mystical-superstitious basis and lasted until the Middle Ages. It was Copernicus's world picture, stress-
ing the infinity of space, that undermined the basis
of A."

This definition is from the encyclopedia *Nordisk Familje-
bok* (Nordic Family Book), published in 1924. Sixty years
ago astrology was regarded as a superstitious nonsense-
phenomenon that had been dying out for four hundred
years. Nobody took it seriously.

That was then. Not long ago I was introduced to a young lady in a Stockholm café. The first thing she asked, after we exchanged names, was which sign of the Zodiac I was born under.

Brief acquaintance

She was in her thirties and, I discovered later, had spent nine years going through primary- and grammar-school education, followed by several years at university. She also had a radical past politically, and seemed to be in full possession of all her intellectual faculties. It is hard to find an excuse for why almost five hundred years of enlightenment and scientific progress had failed to leave any impression at all on her world picture.

"The same as you," I replied. "The moo-cow." That was the full extent of our conversation. It was a brief acquaintance. It may be thought that I am a particularly snooty person, but it is beginning to irritate me that you can barely cross the street without someone tapping you on the shoulder and asking which sign of the Zodiac you were born under. What has been a superstition with no right to exist since the days of Copernicus is now a serious philosophy of life in 1983.

An unknown number

There are today almost five hundred more or less professional astrologists and an unknown number of cheerful amateurs. It is estimated that somewhere in the region of one hundred thousand people in this country consider astrology to be a serious science. Few nonsense-phenomena have experienced such an enormous renaissance in recent decades as has astrology, one of the features of the wave of neo-spirituality that is flowing through the Western world. For ordinary people it can often be difficult to fend off the mystical reasoning being sold by the branch's confidence tricksters. The superstitions are often immersed in long pseudo-scientific argument, referring to sources that are difficult to access, and are presented as incontrovertible facts. An uncritical and frivolous press also provides valuable assistance, and without blinking helps to hammer into its readers totally incredible idiocy.

Even Q

A typical example is the reporting of the remarkable goings-on recently in the Department of Applied Psychology at the University of Lund, where the psychologist Maj Björk recently presented a dissertation entitled "Astrology-Psychology," which is claimed to provide a scientific basis for the belief in astrology. *Aftonbladet* introduced the research in bold type: SHE TESTED HOROSCOPES—THEY WORK. That set the roundabout in motion. *Svenska Dagbladet* presented the thesis as a piece of scientific research, and *Expressen* has invited Maj Björk to write a regular column during the summer on astrology and the Zodiac. Even the radical women's magazine *Kvinnotidningen Q* took the bait and drew attention to Björk's thesis in a daft, uncritical leading article. They were evidently so impressed that a professional astrologer was invited to take part in their jubilee party last spring. According to *Q*'s report, the astrologer was fully booked all evening. I have not renewed my subscription.

Scandal

In the eyes of the general public, without an opportunity to check truth and facts, Björk's thesis seems to be a solid piece of scientific research. Moreover, Björk has announced that she will be using horoscopes when making personality diagnoses of her patients. As if that were not enough, she claims that her dissertation raises questions about the whole basis of our world view and our understanding of reality. Always supposing her dissertation is correct!

But it is not correct. Björk's dissertation is out-and-out pseudo-science, and it is increasingly clear that it is an academic scandal for it to have been passed in the first place.

There is not enough space here to make a detailed criticism of the shortcomings of the dissertation (statistical range, selection method, safety checks, etc.). Let us just say that it fails totally to satisfy the criteria for scientific research, and that it proves nothing at all. The truth seems to be that Björk, who is an astrological believer, has written a dissertation whose purpose is to ratify her own beliefs.

No end to superstition

No newspaper has allocated any space to speak of to critical comments. Needless to say, nor will they be apologizing to their readers for publishing the utter drivel that has been churned out. Neo-spirituality is an insidious phenomenon. It has developed over the last few decades and now comprises no end of superstitions and idiocies, of which astrology is just one instance. Other examples are parapsychology, UFO-logy, occultism, oriental mysticism, biorhythms, the I

Ching, numerology, pyramid-ideology, chiromancy (palmistry), Atlantis cults, variations on quackery, scientology, and much more.

Is neo-spiritualism something to concern us, then? The answer must be that everything expressing itself as a popular movement and involving hundreds of thousands of people must concern us, not least because neo-spiritualism appeals to young people in its use of empty radical emotional phrases. They take delight in accusing traditional science of being conservative and bourgeois, and present themselves as the progressive alternative. But behind that naive façade is an exceptionally reactionary world picture and view of human beings.

Taking your clothes off

Astrology, for instance, strives to present a deterministic world picture, decreed by Fate—i.e. your individual development is somehow fixed in advance, in this case by the position of heavenly bodies and planets at the time of your birth.

Whether you become a drug addict or doctor or docker or stockbroker has nothing to do with your class background, social status, or political opinions. If you have a wretched sex life, this may be because you are a Scorpio and your partner is a Leo, not that the sex education you had at school was rubbish or that the housing shortage means you never have a place where you can take your clothes off.

Common to all aspects of neo-spiritualism is that they argue in favor of a world picture in which there is no possibility of an individual doing anything that can affect his or her environment. It is a passive spirituality, in many cases self-fulfilling.

And so neo-spiritualism offers short cuts to knowledge. Instead of devoting years to study or practical work, you can sit down and be enlightened by meditation, attain happiness by chanting a mantra, or (why not?) discover your true self by means of an L.S.D. trip.

Hard currency

Neo-spiritualism talks about a positive development for the individual. But pseudo-science and superstition have never ever contributed to an improvement in a person's living conditions. Assuming, of course, that you exclude the confidence tricksters who make a profit out of people's gullibility.

Charlatans such as von Däniken and Uri Geller have become millionaires on the basis of fraud. Every self-respecting Swedish publishing house has published several books this year in the field of confidence trickery; and for weekly magazines, investing in the subject is a guarantee of increased circulation. Certain bookshops such as Vattumannen and East&West in Stockholm have specialized in pseudo-science and superstition. Having your personal horoscope delivered by a professional can cost you a few hundred kronor, and Ulla Sallert will churn out a computerized horoscope by mail order for a mere 164 kronor. For 550 kronor you can attend a course in sexual spirituality and Tantra-mysticism with Tolly Burkan and the Livsglädje Täby association (*Joie de vivre* in Täby). For half that price you can also learn how to walk on red-hot coals. In the U.S.A. the market for related gadgetry is red-hot: you can

order a handmade crystal ball for 700 kronor. Gary Eng-
man is cheaper: you can buy your daily horoscope in *Aftonbladet* for 2.50.

The young lady I mentioned at the beginning of this article is unfortunately not a one-off isolated phenomenon. It is
not difficult to become a modern hermit once you have lost
your way in the neo-spiritualist jungle. It is harder to find
your way out again.

*This article was written under Stieg Larsson's pseudonym,
Severin.*

A DEFEAT FOR DEMOCRACY

Expo, previously unpublished

Saturday, November 8, 1997, was a turning point for the postwar Swedish Nazi movement—110 uniformed neo-Nazis marched through central Stockholm, from Norra Bantorget to Medborgarplatsen. The first advertised and openly anti-Jewish demonstration in Sweden since the Second World War was a fact. There was a lot of discussion about the event in the mass media. With good reason.

Since the Second World War there has been such a strong taboo about openly expressed hatred of the Jews in Western Europe that even the most fanatical neo-Nazi groups have maintained quite a low profile on anti-Semitic questions.

Immigrants, homosexuals and other political enemies have replaced the Jews as the key objects of hatred. Anything else would have been unthinkable after Auschwitz.

But this does not mean that Nazism has jettisoned anti-Semitism, merely that raising it in public has been tactically inadvisable. Throughout the postwar period the Nazi movement has continued to pursue anti-Semitic propaganda. At internal meetings and at ex-servicemen's reunions there has never been any doubt about who is the enemy number one.

Since the end of the 1970s one particular branch of the Nazi movement has devoted itself to "historical revisionism"—rewriting history by erasing memories of Auschwitz and denying that the Holocaust, the extermination of six million Jews, ever took place. Thanks to Swedish activists such as Ditlieb Felderer, Ahmed Rami,[1] Göran Holming[2] and their international cronies, revisionism has acquired an increasingly important ideological role.

Newly awoken anti-Semitism

At the end of the 1970s undisguised hatred of the Jews once again became prominent in the international Nazi movement, not least in the U.S.A., where small but ideologically significant groups such as the Aryan Nations and National Alliance made no secret of their aims. What was needed was a "white revolution without pardon," and the total extermination of the world's Jews.

It was several years before these impulses took root in Sweden, but since the late 1980s hatred of the Jews has once again become the core of the Nazi message. Vitt Ariskt

Motstånd was the first Swedish organization to declare "war on Z.O.G."—the Zionist Occupation Government.

When white-power music broke through in 1993 it became easier to spread racist propaganda, and anti-Semitism became an important factor in the texts.

But it was not until November 8 that the National Socialist Front (N.S.F.) marched through the streets of Stockholm and made everything plain. The N.S.F., led on that day by their spokesman Björn Björkqvist from Gotland, had several objectives for their demonstration.

Crush democracy

The N.S.F. put down an unambiguous marker to the effect that it was time to "stop pretending." The main slogan during the march was "Crush democracy"—something no Swedish Nazi group had earlier dared to voice.

This was the opposite of what they usually say: in public the neo-Nazis have always presented themselves as ultra-democratic. The Nordiska Rikspartiet (N.R.P.—Nordic National Party), for example, has continuously complained that the established political parties are "undemocratic" in that, for instance, they will not allow the N.R.P. to hire rooms in community centers such as Folkets hus (the People's House).

The reality of course is that the only common aim of all fascist parties in all countries and at all times has been to "crush democracy." The particular kind of democracy is irrelevant—bourgeois parliamentarianism, socialist soviets and communal independence are merely different aspects of the same thing in the eyes of Nazism: the attempt by the Jewish conspiracy to destabilize the white Aryan race.

The second important marker laid down by the N.S.F. during the march through Stockholm was the claim that the N.S.F. is a "workers' party." This is yet again a return to the ideals of the Brownshirts from the 1930s.

Nazis with self-confidence

The third—and possibly most important—marker was that the N.S.F. is not afraid of either the police or anti-fascist counter-demonstrators.

The N.S.F. had sought police permission for the demonstration, and been turned down. Now they were showing as clearly as you like that they couldn't care less what the police or the authorities say or think. The message was that whenever the N.S.F. choose to march through the streets of Stockholm, they will do so. They regarded the fact that a group of anti-racists intended to hold a counter-demonstration as no more than a minor irritation.

Before the march the N.S.F. made it known that they would carry out their demonstration at the advertised time. They intended to set out from Norra Bantorget and march through Stockholm and then hold a public meeting. The police ban was irrelevant, and if anti-racists tried to stop them they would "beat the shit out of them."

The N.S.F. did exactly what they said they would do. They marched from Norra Bantorget to Central Station, where they held a fifteen-minute public meeting, then processed to the Södermalm district. Neither the police nor the anti-racists could stop them—albeit for different reasons. The only contribution made by the police during the demonstration was to provide an escort service for the neo-Nazis. The behavior of the police has since come in for brutal but justified criticism.

The neo-Nazi demonstration set off from a place with classical political significance—Branting Park, named after the "father" of social democracy in Sweden, fifty meters from the Swedish trade union headquarters. The counter-demonstration was organized by Föreningen Hasans Vänner (Hasan's Friends Association),[3] which amassed some two hundred anti-racists, mainly young people.

And so, for a few hours, it was these young people who formed our society's only line of defense against a collection of Nazis whose purpose was to abolish democracy.

This article was written for the December 1997 issue of Expo, *which was never published.*

Notes

1. See note on Felderer and Rami on p. 55.
2. Göran Holming was a notorious Holocaust denier in the 1990s. In 1997 he was fired from his position as major after he sent an anti-Semitic letter to an elderly Jewish man. Holming was for many years active in the circles of Radio Islam, claiming among other things that Hitler had never planned to exterminate the Jews.
3. Hasans Vänner was an anti-racist organization formed in Stockholm in 1992 after a series of assassination attempts on immigrants.

RESPONSE TO ANTI-DEMOCRATIC PROPAGANDA

Expo 1—2/2002
Co-authored with Mikael Ekman

The Sweden Democrats describe themselves as a democratic party that is ruthlessly harassed and persecuted by an anti-democratic system—politicians, the mass media and state authorities. That strategy—and accompanying rhetoric—is copied from the Front National in France and similar parties. And the response should be the same in Sweden as it is in France. *Expo* now offers some of those responses to the most common arguments put forward by the Sweden Democrats.

The Sweden Democrats are not allowed to participate in the election campaign on the same terms as other political parties!

This is a political lie. All parties operate under exactly the same conditions and compete for exactly the same voters. The Swedish constitutional right of free speech and freedom of organization applies to all Swedish citizens without exception.

There are no constitutional obstacles preventing the Sweden Democrats from taking part in the election: they have access to the same opportunities to publish election manifestos, leaflets, magazines; the same opportunities to produce local radio broadcasts and publish material on the Internet as any other party. It is true that the Sweden Democrats do not feature in the mass media and on television to the same extents as, let us say, the Social Democrats, the Left Party or the Moderates [the Swedish Conservative Party]. The Sweden Democrats are a marginal party, and it is entirely appropriate that parties represented in parliament and with significantly greater support among voters should attract proportionately more attention.

The Sweden Democrats are gagged and suppressed by the political establishment!

This claim is nonsense. It is true, however, that none of the democratic parties is particularly interested in debating with a marginal, racist party that subscribes to conspiracy theories and conducts hate campaigns against democratic politicians.

The Sweden Democrats are not allowed to hire rooms in community centers such as the People's House or the Workers' Educational Association. This proves that Sweden is a sham democracy!

Democracy does not exist purely for the benefit of racist parties. The A.B.F. (Workers' Educational Association) and other educational associations do have democratic rights. They are independent institutions with the right to decide which groups they will admit into their premises as guests.

Democracy gives rights to opponents of the Sweden Democrats—in this case the right to refuse to let rooms to racist organizations. If the Sweden Democrats want to hold public meetings there is nothing to stop them from doing so in their own premises.

They can't afford it? Ah, well, that is sad—but hardly a problem for the A.B.F. and other educational organizations. Every newly formed party seeking the support of voters operates under precisely the same marginal conditions.

The Sweden Democrats are subjected to censorship in public debate, and their letters to the editor are not published by local newspapers!

This claim is a political lie. Articles and letters to the editor from the Sweden Democrats are published regularly in local newspapers. But in any case, the same argument applies as in the previous repudiation: democracy is not merely for the benefit of racist parties. Swedish newspapers are independent institutions whose editors are free to choose what material their publications will carry.

Most letters editors are not interested in publishing contributions from groups manifestly devoted to conspiracy theories and who claim, among other things, that the terrorist attack on the World Trade Center was "partly financed by the Swedish government." This is not an issue about democracy but rather an example of common sense being displayed by editors.

The Sweden Democrats are a normal democratic party!
The Sweden Democrats are a racist, anti-democratic party dedicated to conspiracy theories. There is no such thing as "democratic racism"—the fact that the party conducts racist campaigns and stirs up contempt for and discriminatory attitudes towards sexual minorities also justifies the party being labelled as anti-democratic.

The Sweden Democrats are not against immigration, but only want to criticize Swedish immigration policies!
From the very start racism and xenophobia have been the cement that holds the party together. Over the years the party has conducted crude hate campaigns and tried to cultivate the myth that immigrants in general are "potential criminals," "spreaders of HIV" and "potential rapists." The constant intention has been to cultivate an attitude of contempt towards people whose skin is a different color.

The Sweden Democrats oppose immigration from non-European countries and their aim is the repatriation—in other words the expulsion—of immigrants.

The leader of the party, Mikael Jansson, has stated that they are not talking about voluntary repatriation: "We are in favor of the compulsory repatriation of all asylum seekers from foreign cultures who have entered Sweden since 1970." The Sweden Democrats thereby advocate a doctrine that can only be called "ethnic cleansing in Sweden."

The Sweden Democrats are not interested in the color of a person's skin; we believe that "It doesn't matter whether adopted children are white or black"!

The Sweden Democrats' manifesto states specifically that the adoption of children from outside Europe should cease. Since children brought up in Sweden from an early age will be to all intents and purposes Swedish from a cultural point of view, this stipulation can refer only to skin color.

Discussion of the immigration problem in Sweden is suppressed, and criticism of immigration policies is not permitted!

This claim too is nonsense but is raised over and over again by the Sweden Democrats and other racist groups.

In fact the immigration question is one of the most widely debated issues in Swedish politics over the last thirty to forty years. Immigration has been discussed by all the democratic parties, by the government, the parliament and local government institutions, within trade unions and employers' organizations, within state authorities, in schools, universities, workplaces and voluntary organizations. The upshot of these deliberations is that there is remarkable unity within Swedish public institutions to the effect that our country supports the U.N. Charter of Human Rights, directives from the U.N. Displaced Persons Commission and other international agreements: immigrants are welcome in Sweden.

On the other hand, the precise form that immigration takes—what numbers, at what rate, how immigrants should be received and treated and how the integration process should proceed—is under continual discussion, and there can be many differences of opinion. It is not racist to criticize the immigration process, nor to argue that immigration policies have serious shortcomings.

Racism is on the increase in our country. It is out of concern for the welfare of immigrants that the Sweden Democrats want them to "return home"!

Immigrants usually politely decline assistance from the Sweden Democrats. Ever since the party was founded as a campaigning organization entitled "Keep Sweden Swedish" in 1979, it has cultivated racism and conducted xenophobic campaigns. After spending many years encouraging xenophobia, the Sweden Democrats now use "increasing racism" as an excuse for repatriating immigrants.

The Sweden Democrats are the party for those who are in favor of law and order in our society!

The Sweden Democrats have far and away more criminals among their numbers than any other party. *Expo*'s investigation into 330 "leading Sweden Democrats" (people who had either been members of the national party council or submitted themselves as Sweden Democrat candidates in an election) between 1988 and 1998 showed that more than 23 percent of them had been found guilty of criminal activity.

That is almost twice the highest-known figure for immigrant criminality, which shows that just over 12 percent of all immigrants have been convicted of crimes. This figure has been criticized as exaggerated. It is normally reckoned that about 6 percent of all Swedes will sooner or later be convicted of a crime, and that the corresponding figure for immigrants is only slightly higher at about 7 percent.

Criminality within the Sweden Democrats covers all categories—insurance fraud, cruelty to animals, theft, assaults on women, grievous bodily harm, drink-driving, embezzlement, arson, and so on.

There are criminals in all political parties!
Very true. But the conduct of normal politicians is scrutinized by the Parliamentary Standing Committee on the Constitution, the National Audit Office, local auditors, opposing parties, public prosecutors, police authorities, and not least by the mass media. Politicians in normal parties who are convicted of crimes are disqualified more or less straight away.

The crime statistics for the Sweden Democrats are in no way comparable with the situation in normal democratic parties.

The Sweden Democrats have no contacts with anti-democratic or right-wing extremists abroad!
The Sweden Democrats are members of the cooperation organization Euro-Nat and hence one of the signatories of the "Young European Nationalists' Manifesto."[1] Among other signatories are the racist party Vlaams Blok[2] in Belgium, the anti-Semitic România Mare[3] from Romania and the neo-fascist Forza Nuova[4] from Italy. The foreign organization closest to the party is the French Front National.[5]

The Sweden Democrats are Not Nazis!

No, but on the other hand nobody has suggested that the Sweden Democrats are a neo-Nazi party. There is, however, plenty of evidence that over the years the relationship with Nazism has been fluid, that Sweden Democrat members have moved to or from Nazi sects, or have been members of both.

The Sweden Democrats were founded originally as the racist campaigning organization Bevara Sverige Svenskt (Keep Sweden Swedish) in 1979. Several of the founders have a background of neo-Nazi group membership, and over the years a large proportion of the party executive have been linked with neo-Nazi movements.

The claim by Expo that the Sweden Democrats have had Nazis among their leaders is a lie! There have been a few cases of short-lived youthful folly, and a few infiltrators when the party was first launched.

At the beginning of the 1990s just over half the members of the S.D. party executive had links with openly Nazi groups. In 1995, 42 percent of the party executive still had Nazi links. Then a purge was begun. Yet some of the youthful folly has continued for rather a long time: as recently as 2001 several leading members were expelled in connection with the formation of the National Democrats. They were accused of being—Nazis.

Notes

1. Euro-Nat was a network of nationalist parties in Europe which grew out of a collaboration between parties that had tried to

form a right-wing group in the European Parliament during the '90s.

2. Vlaams Blok was founded in 1978 as an alliance between two nationalist right-wing parties. The party called for an independent Flanders and reduced immigration, and gained rapid success. It was banned in 2004, when the Belgian court decided that all three non-profit organizations connected to the Vlaams Blok had violated the 1981 anti-racism law.

3. România Mare was founded in 1991 by Corneliu Vadim Tudor, who still leads the party. It has often been represented in both the national parliament and the European Parliament. The party has several times been accused of having distributed anti-Semitic propaganda.

4. Forza Nuova is a radical right-wing party led by Roberti Fiore. It has not generally been successful in elections, but nevertheless plays an important role in building alliances between right-wing extremist groups across Europe.

5. The Front National is one of the most famous right-wing parties in Europe. Founded in 1972, it got its big break in the 1984 elections to the European Parliament. Front National was for many years led by Jean-Marie Le Pen, who has now been replaced by his daughter, Marine Le Pen.

CRACKS BEHIND A UNIFIED FAÇADE

www.expo.se

May 6, 2003

"The Sweden Democrats are more united than ever" is the not entirely true headline on the website of their journal *SD-Kuriren* following the party's annual general meeting last weekend.

The A.G.M. was supposed to take place in Örebro, but was moved to the Trollhättan community center after their Örebro booking was cancelled. As always, it is difficult to work out what actually happened at the A.G.M. from the party's own terse report. According to *SD-Kuriren*, the meeting was characterized by "solidarity and a go-ahead spirit," and a conviction that they will win parliamentary seats at the next election.

Mikael Jansson was elected for a new term as party leader. This was not unexpected; any attempt to put up an alternative candidate in the current situation would run the risk of starting a civil war within the party. The fact is that behind *SD-Kuriren*'s claims of unity there are very real differences of opinion. Manning the trenches on one side are a number of party veterans who advocate "traditional" policies. Opposing them are "innovators" who call the veterans the "bunker mafia" and demand something as basic as an internal democratic system for members that actually works.

The bunker mafia are keen to claim responsibility for last year's electoral successes. But in fact it is the new arrivals who are responsible for most of the progress. When the party started to grow, most of the new members were not tainted by membership of the traditional "nationalist" movement and did not have a murky past in some obscure sect. On the contrary, people appeared who had roots in traditional democratic parties. The chairman of S.D.-Borås, Kristoffer Heller, for example, used to be a member of the Swedish Conservative Party's youth wing; and the party's strongman in Kävlinge, Kenneth Sandberg, had many years' experience as a local council representative of the Left Party in the days when it added the designation "Communists" in brackets after the party name. For newcomers like them, *Realpolitik* is more important than the more esoteric aspects the S.D.'s bunker mafia have been advocating since the party was launched.

As a result, since the progress made in last year's elections the bunker mafia have realized to their horror that their position is increasingly under fire and questioned by the younger generation. The veterans are aware that the party needs new blood in order to survive and grow—but they are not keen on the lack of respect and internal criticism that go hand in hand with their party's expansion.

Ideologically speaking, there are no dramatic differences between the factions—not, at least, in their attitude to immigrants and Muslims—but the newcomers insist on the same levels of competence and professionalism from the party's functionaries as are displayed by the "usual parties." Internally, there has been savage criticism of individual party activists in positions of responsibility.

As far as the internal power struggle is concerned, the result of this year's A.G.M. can probably be described as a draw. The elections for the party's executive board did not produce any startling change, which means that the bunker mafia are still sitting pretty, more or less.

Much of the internal criticism has been directed at the party's deputy leader, Johan Rinderheim, who was previously a board member of the hard-pressed local division in Haninge, and since last autumn has been a board member in Nynäshamn. Rinderheim was demoted one rung down the ladder and is now assistant deputy chairman. He was replaced by Björn Söder, who is now deputy chairman of the party and in line to be made party leader at the next A.G.M.

Söder has made his attitude clear by demanding that the party's board member in Askersund, Björn Lennartsson, should be expelled for saying what he thinks—in his case a series of crude racist attacks.

Changing the party leader before the next election is one of the prerequisites. Jansson causes irritation internally for not reacting to proposals from reformers and for seldom taking the initiative for anything at all.

The most serious loss for the S.D. is of course that their well-known luminary Sten Andersson from Malmö is no longer a member of the party's executive board. He has claimed "personal reasons" for not standing for reelection, but he is also one of those who have been targeted by snipers.

Among those who have disappeared from the scene is Anders Westergren from Höör. Westergren featured in a video film for the television program "Insider," which demonstrated how he had hired out land he owns for a meeting organized by the National Socialist Front, and taken part in the meeting, at which a bonfire was made of "Jewish literature." Per Emanuelsson, from the former core of the party in Gothenburg, has also disappeared.

The A.G.M. of 2003 has by no means solved the Sweden Democrats' internal problems, and the party now faces a period of uncertainty. If the squabbles are not resolved the party could fall apart, and those highly desirable seats in parliament could disappear below the horizon. It is already apparent that there has been practically no activity at all in many districts since the election. This is the case in Mölndal, for instance, where the party won two seats in the local elections last autumn; and according to democratic local councilors in Nynäshamn, not much has been heard from Johan Rinderheim since he was elected last autumn. The main thrust of the party at the moment comes from Skåne, but activists there have had their own traditional differences for many years.

Ironically enough the S.D.'s anti-E.M.U. (Economic and Monetry Union) campaign, *Försvara kronan!* (Defend the krona!), was launched in Trollhättan at the same time as the A.G.M. The party had originally intended to launch it on Engelbrekt's Day in Stockholm the previous week, but they were outmaneuvered by the National Democrats.

THE PARTY THAT'S OVER THE LIMIT

www.expo.se
May 15, 2003

It will be fascinating to study the development of the Sweden Democrats during the coming year, if only from a cultural-anthropology perspective.

This year's party congress is over and done with, and the *S.D.-Kuriren*'s home page proclaimed proudly that the Sweden Democrats were more united than ever before. Two weeks later Mats Strandberg deserted. He chose to transfer his allegiance to their arch-enemy the National Democrats (N.D.), who are only too happy to snap up any crumbs that fall from the S.D.'s table. And at around the same time the N.D. announced that the S.D.'s local activist in Karlskrona, Christer Carlsson, had also gone over to the N.D.

Carlsson's desertion is no great loss. To be sure, for a short time he was a local party organizer for the S.D.; but he is undoubtedly a second-rate performer of no political significance. On the other hand, Mats Strandberg's going is quite a different kettle of fish. He was one of two deputy chairmen of the Stockholm division, and elected to that post as recently as March this year. He is not one of your usual oddballs, but a grown-up person with a well-organized private life, a family, a job, and he wears a suit and tie—exactly the sort of person the S.D. want to show off as the house-trained and decorous backbone of the party.

To make things worse, during the last two years the S.D.-Stockholm have lost so many of their activists that any normal party would be licking its wounds. Among the deserters are the likes of Henrik Ehnmark, for many years a well-known personality on local radio; also Tomas Johansson, the ideologue who put everything to rights after an earlier factional struggle with the Hembygdspartiet (Homestead Party); and Sven Davidsson, who was one of the S.D.'s founders. In addition, several of the next generation's key activists have deserted from the youth wing of the Sweden Democrats

There is good reason to state that the bloodletting has been so profuse that the Stockholm division of the S.D. is hemorrhaging to death.

None of this seems to worry the party leadership, who simply shrug and dismiss the N.D. as a neo-Nazi party; they also think it a good thing that some two-thirds of their own

Stockholm division have disappeared from view. For whatever reason, the party organizer claims that the party is not
"busy at a meeting," as *Expo* carelessly reported after talking
to him yesterday.

The Sweden Democrats make a big effort to assure journalists and politicians that they "have now become a house-
trained party." They claim that the various neo-Nazis and
criminals who have been members of the party over the
years had merely succumbed to "the follies of youth." They
like to draw comparisons with the Social Democrats, who,
they allege, had anarchists among their leaders at the beginning of the last century. And every time they go through a
serious schism, they claim confidently that the youthful follies have been overcome and the party has become democratic. They recited the same mantra when their two former
deputy leaders defected to the National Socialist Front; and
they repeated it after the split with the Homestead Party in
1996. And it was the same story after the catastrophe with
the National Democrats in 2001.

It is all the more important to understand the reasons for
the split. The National Democrats came into being in the
summer of 2001 after Anders Steen and Tor Paulsson were
expelled from the S.D.

At the time, Anders Steen was a member of the party
executive representing Haninge, one of the party's eight
board members and hence somebody the party leadership would be reluctant to lose. Tor Paulsson had been
the party organizer and was regarded internally as the one
who had devised the strategy for the 1998 election. In other
words, it was not a question of two second-raters who were

summarily expelled from their posts at the summit of the party and accused of being Nazis, and attempting to create a party within a party.

The S.D. leadership probably thought the affair would soon pass and be forgotten; but dissatisfaction with party leader Jansson was so widespread that a large proportion of the Stockholm division rebelled. Instead of disappearing into the sunset, Steen was nominated as leader of a new party, with Paulsson as his chief whip. The remarkable thing is that it was almost impossible to distinguish any marked political or ideological difference between the two factions. The S.D. had discovered that Steen and Paulsson, who the previous year had been key figures in the development of S.D. policies, were in fact "Nazis"—but both factions continued to pursue more or less the same policies.

It is true that since then the N.D. has become even more of a Nazi party after absorbing a large number of activists, mainly from the National Youth movement; and the party has good relations with similar groups in the European Union. Among their members are several well-known propagandists who had previously been democratic anti-Semites in the S.D., but who, according to the S.D., are now anti-democratic anti-Semites in the N.D. But there is no yawning gap between the policies of the N.D. and the S.D. Both parties state that they are "nationalist," that they hate the E.U., that they are in favor of apartheid, that they want an ethnically cleansed Sweden and oppose all forms of immigration.

The real reasons for the split were personal antagonism and good old power struggles. Among the S.D. activists there was (and still is) widespread dissatisfaction with the leadership. This is especially true in Stockholm, where the veterans Torbjörn Kastell and Johan Rinderheim and others have dictated policy in such a way that they have earned the nickname of the bunker mafia.

It is symptomatic that when Mats Strandberg defected to the N.D. he gave seven different reasons for doing so. These included "unsatisfactory social competence," "faulty organization," "fear of being frank," "excessive intake of alcohol" and "failure to grasp the realities of the economy."

Take note: nowhere in his defection document does Strandberg criticize the policies of the S.D. He is disillusioned because a gang of social incompetents sits around every evening in the party bunker in the Södermalm district of Stockholm drinking beer and achieving a higher percentage of blood alcohol than of support among the voters.

Moreover, the comrades in the party secretariat are so secretive that even members of the Stockholm executive board are not allowed into the bunker for "security reasons." Following the split with the N.D., security has been tightened even more. But it is fascinating to note that the sister of one of the N.D.'s leaders is employed as a domestic worker by the S.D. party secretariat.

The other day *Expo* received an e-mail from a former Sweden Democrat, wondering what we would do if the S.D. succeeded in making themselves respectable after getting rid of the six to eight prominent members who had been causing problems. I replied to the effect that I was not holding my breath and expecting the S.D. to become a democratic party, and that rather more expulsions than the somewhat hopeful number he gave would be necessary.

The key question is rather what the party's "innovators" will do next. Jan Milld from Haninge, who joined in the summer of 2002, has already delivered a devastating critique of the lack of democracy within the party. We published extracts from his letter in the last issue of *Expo*. How long will he remain a party member? And what will Sten Andersson in Malmö do next? He was "assured" by the party leadership that the S.D.'s youthful follies were now over and done with before he defected from the Swedish Conservative Party. How long will he stay?

An even more interesting question: where will they go to after the S.D.? They have burned their bridges, and no normal party will be willing to take them back.

And another interesting question: where will Mats Strandberg go next when he discovers that his move from the S.D. to the N.D. failed to satisfy his hopes? As a member of the S.D., Strandberg made a name for himself as a supporter of the E.M.U. He has now joined a party known for its ferocious campaigns against the E.M.U.

THE SWEDEN DEMOCRATS AND
THEIR DEFECTOR

www.expo.se

June 3, 2004

"Tommy Funebo is a destructive person," fumes the Sweden Democrats' leader, Mikael Jansson. That was more or less Jansson's only comment to the media when his former national party organizer defected with a resounding bang from the Sweden Democrats and handed over several thousand pages of party documents to their arch-enemy, *Expo*. These documents form the basis of the book *Sverigedemokraterna från insidan* (The Sweden Democrats from the Inside), to be published this week by *Expo* and Hjalmarson & Högberg Förlag.

Yes, Tommy Funebo can no doubt be considered a "destructive person" from Mikael Jansson's point of view.

But to the rest of society he seems to be regarded as a person with a considerable amount of civic courage. For the first time since the Sweden Democrats were founded one of their leading figures has had enough, and spoken his mind.

In the middle of the 1990s I spent an evening talking to someone who had defected from the Sweden Democrats in connection with the battle against the Hembygdspartiet (Homestead Party). Unlike most other defectors, he chose not to join the Homestead Party instead, on the grounds that it was a neo-Nazi party and he was not a Nazi. Rather late in the day he had realized that he was not a Sweden Democrat either. His analysis was simple: the Sweden Democrats were not a democratic party and hence it was not the place for him. He was a democrat—albeit an arch-conservative one.

This defector was not a party organizer, nor was he a member of the executive committee; but he had a position that gave him a fair amount of insight into what went on behind the scenes. The story he had to tell about daily life in Sweden's "most democratic party"—this was a time when half of the executive committee were undisguised Nazis—was rather bizarre. I suggested he should go public with his story, but he preferred not to do so.

The reason was straightforward: he was afraid of the consequences. He was afraid that doing so would lead to threats and even violence against him. He knew exactly who were the party's torpedoes (some of them are still there in leading positions), and he knew what had happened to other defectors or internal critics.

Some of those critics, including one of the party's founders, had been subjected to long hate campaigns that even threatened his parents when two leading members were seen skulking in the bushes outside their house. Another critic of the party who was well known for his local radio broadcasts in Stockholm was beaten up so badly that he ended up in hospital. The defector I was talking to had just become a father, and did not want to expose himself to risks of that kind. That is understandable. He took the step of supplying information, then disappeared silently into the wings.

By pure coincidence I happened to bump into him about a year ago. He is now a member of the Moderates, the Swedish Conservative Party, and feels very much at home there. He lives in a small provincial town and has various political responsibilities. Meeting me was a reminder of his circumstances ten years ago. He looked embarrassed. As we were drinking coffee, he showed me photographs of his daughter. He shook his head and said he failed to understand how he had once been so stupid as to become a member of a "nationalist" party.

"Nobody knows I used to be a member of the Sweden Democrats in those days," he said. "I've never mentioned it to a soul. I'm scared that it might come out one of these days. That would be a catastrophe for me."

"Why?"

"Because they would obviously put a slant on it in such a way that it would damage my political activities and the party I'm now a member of."

O.K., that is an understandable explanation. It goes with the territory of being a defector. But I do not believe that this particular defector would suffer dramatic problems. He is still—as he puts it—conservative, but he is not a racist, and above all he has never been a Nazi. For a few years as a teenager he was a member of the Sweden Democrats. He cannot even remember why he joined, apart from the fact that a friend of his was a member and that there was always plenty of booze at the parties organized by their mates in the party.

Having defected from the Sweden Democrats Tommy Funebo is in an unenviable situation. He is—he himself says—conservative, but he is not a racist. He is also a democrat, which means that for several years he was a member of the wrong party. He is out of work and has anything but bright prospects of finding in the foreseeable future a workplace where colleagues will be prepared to accept a defector from a notorious nationalist party.

Why did he join the Sweden Democrats?

That is something he is probably unable to explain, even to himself. That is usually the case. People join a party like the Sweden Democrats for one of two reasons.

Either you are fundamentally undemocratic and believe in some fascist or nationalist ideal, such as anti-Semitism or racism. Or you are not like that but feel alienated by the normal democratic parties—the established society somehow falls short of what you think it should be like, or you feel it fails to serve the best interests of its citizens. I suspect this may well be close to the reason why Tommy Funebo joined the Sweden Democrats.

The fascinating thing about defectors is that they nearly all tell identical stories. They get carried away for some reason they can barely explain to themselves retrospectively—they were attracted by a sticky label or they read a pamphlet or they had a friend who persuaded them to join the movement. They join the party with good intentions and fail to see that in fact they have landed in a political sect in which entirely different rules, codes and regulations apply compared with life in normal society. The bizarre becomes everyday fare. Hate politics becomes routine. Conspiracy theories become the norm.

Then comes a period of adaptation. It is during this time that the wheat is separated from the chaff. Those who are unable to adapt disappear quite soon. Those who try to adapt and to live up to demands affecting their behavior, their views and internal rhetoric can stay on. They then often need to do violence to themselves and their own views.

Tommy Funebo says that with hindsight he thinks he has been naive; convinced by assurances and promises, he preferred to believe that any blemishes he detected in the party were remains of unpleasantnesses that were in the process of being erased. This self-deception works only so far, but sooner or later a time comes when the hesitant activist has to make a decision. As far as Funebo was concerned it meant that he was forced to resign from the Sweden Democrats. It was the only decent thing to do.

It is normal for defectors to disappear silently into the wings. But Funebo chose the difficult way, and it exposed him to the hatred of the Sweden Democrats (and other nationalist groups). He cannot tell a lie. He tells the truth about what he experienced in the Sweden Democrats.

Another difference between Tommy and usual defectors is that he can back up his claims with documentary evidence—minutes of committee meetings, budget proposals, organization plans, internal e-mails and even tape-recordings of top-secret crisis meetings.

Funebo's defection will leave its mark on the party structure of the Sweden Democrats. It will be a year or even longer before the full consequences become evident.

One result is that all the claims made by critics of the party—including *Expo*—can now be documented using the party's own papers. When we maintain that the S.D. is an anti-democratic nationalist party, that claim can now be proved.

Another result is that we now have invaluable information about what goes on behind the political sect's impenetrable façade—things that the party leadership want to hide from ordinary members at any price. There is something wrong with a party in which the tone of internal discussions sinks to a level like the following description of an employee working in its head office: "[He is] lazy, a drunken sot, cowardly, mean, introverted, completely lacking in initiative, wasteful, asocial, his personal hygiene leaves a lot to be desired and he has a condescending attitude towards anybody who isn't a boozer or a committee member . . ." But he is a nationalist. That is what matters as far as the party is concerned.

Funebo says that if ordinary members realized how their party was run behind the scenes, they would be furious. Which is why ordinary members do not have such insight into what is surely Sweden's most *un*democratic party. If they want to achieve that insight, they will have to read the books that *Expo* publishes. And that is why Mikael Jansson calls Tommy Funebo a "destructive person."

N.D. SIDELINED

www.expo.se
August 27, 2004

News of the split in the ranks of the National Democrats was received in *Expo*'s editorial office with professional calm and restraint. The National Democrats (N.D.) were founded in the summer of 2001, and split in the summer of 2004. The obvious comment to make about this news is to wonder why it took so long.

Expo has kept an eye on the National Democrats' activities, without attaching any serious importance to them. Compared with the Sweden Democrats, the National Democrats have been more entertaining, to be sure; but it has always been the S.D. that were the significant party.

It was obvious that the N.D. would split from the moment it was launched. The party has always been based on irreconcilable opposites: its ideology and activists have advocated Nazism while its rhetoric and official principles have sought to claim that the party is democratic. There is no such thing as "democratic Nazism," and hence the question has always been when the intrinsic differences would reach a critical level.

The National Democrats were founded as a result of a split in the Sweden Democrats. The split was not ideological—there was no significant difference between the two factions—but had to do with personal prestige, power struggles and attitudes towards tactics in their practical work. The strategy of the Sweden Democrats has been to establish themselves as a "democratic" party—the word even occurs in their name.

The equation was simple: in order to achieve political success the Sweden Democrats needed to acquire support from voters who were dissatisfied with the political establishment but did not consider themselves to be Nazis or "nationalists." As long as the S.D. appeared to be a traditional Nazi organization with skinheads and uniformed lunatics to the fore, the party scared off all potential voters. When Mikael Jansson took over as leader in 1995, one of his first actions was to ban the wearing of uniforms at public meetings. Since then the party has gradually sidelined the most obvious madmen and militants and replaced them with elegantly dressed and comparatively house-trained activists, including both young people and pensioners. The crudest racial propaganda has been toned down and replaced by a reasonable and uncontroversial party program.

This tactic produced results at the polls. In 1998 the party increased its votes from 13,000 to 20,000, and it broke through in 2002 with 76,000 votes and fifty local council seats. This made the Sweden Democrats the biggest party in Sweden with no representation in parliament.

The disadvantage with the tactic was that although the party attracted more votes, it also caused dissatisfaction within the hard core of faithful servants and activists who had slaved away to produce leaflets and spread propaganda. These veterans had joined a neo-Nazi party after all, and had never doubted where they stood on the nationalist scale; but suddenly the party program seemed unrecognizable to them, to be "liberalized," and nobody dared to speak his mind anymore. And so the hard core of activists broke away and in August 2001 opened up their own shop, as it were, in the form of the National Democrats.

The National Democrats collected both party veterans and faithful servants such as the founder of the S.D., Sven Davidsson, and Tomas Johansson and Henrik Ehnmark. Their front man was Anders Steen, and the former S.D. national organizer Tor Paulsson was the driving force behind the split. The defectors were also supported by a large group within the S.D. Youth Association and a few leading activists in the provinces; but on the whole the N.D. was a Stockholm phenomenon based in Haninge.

In its propaganda the N.D. has always tried to present itself as a party for the whole of Sweden, and a number of regional branches have quickly been set up, although they exist more on paper than in reality. The party has also placed a lot of stress on propaganda and public meetings and events, urging members to travel and show themselves in various places throughout the country.

The party's strength has always been that the people it attracted from the Sweden Democrats were some of the most enterprising and motivated activists—so it was relatively easy for Tor Paulsson to wield the party whip and insist on members travelling to meetings and rallies. This can be done for as long as enthusiasm remains high, but comparatively quickly even the most enthusiastic members grow tired of street marches.

When the National Democrats were well established, just in time for the 2002 elections, they came up against the next problem. By then more or less everybody who wanted to defect from the Sweden Democrats had already done so, and hence the N.D. had to look elsewhere for new recruits. They turned more and more to the traditional Nazi movement, not least the National Youth.

By doing that, as there is no such thing as "democratic Nazism," it was guaranteed that the party would have problems. *Expo*'s mole, Daniel Poohl, who followed the party closely for some months after it was formed, concluded from the start that there was a significant proportion of Nazis among the membership. The N.D. was nothing more than an attempt to found a Nazi party with a "democratic" profile.

The first problem occurred in connection with the 2002 election. The Sweden Democrats became the country's biggest party outside parliament, while the N.D. had to be content with a mere four local council seats and a tenth of the number of votes received by the S.D. Even though this had been more or less inevitable, it seems to have been a rude awakening for many of the activists, who had reckoned on considerably more success. Above all they had expected the Sweden Democrats to collapse.

The National Democrats' room for maneuver also shrank dramatically. There could hardly be much in the way of local council activities when they had seats in only two constituencies, and the credibility of the party's alleged democratic standing was undermined because it could operate only within the framework of traditional Nazism. So the party could appear only at such events as the Salem March.[1] The few new recruits the N.D. had acquired were mainly anti-Semitic propagandists. The party's "successes" became increasingly empty rhetoric on its website and self-congratulatory campaigns at occasional venues.

Needless to say, when a militant right-wing extremist party turns up in a provincial town, it causes a stir. Several local politicians have looked on in dismay when the N.D. has visited their backyard—Norrtälje, Mölndal and elsewhere.

Whenever we at *Expo* have delivered lectures or held discussions with political party committees in various communities we have been forced to dampen down this dismay. It is true that the National Democrats are not backward in coming forward and have a group of activists who are extremely energetic—but in fact it is mainly saber rattling and nothing to worry about. The National Democrats are here today and will be gone tomorrow, swallowed up by the ranting of nationalists.

This attitude is also reflected on *Expo*'s home page and in the journal itself. We have reported important incidents when the National Democrats have been involved— such as the attack on Pride[2] in 2003—but when it comes to political influence the Sweden Democrats have always been of much greater significance. That is where the most important anti-democratic pondlife flourishes, as is clear not least in defector Tommy Funebo's description of the situation inside the S.D.

It may be found amusing to note that the National Democrats managed to turn even that into a conspiracy theory: as *Expo* has often ignored the N.D. and reported on the S.D. to a much greater extent, this must be a sign that *Expo* "has been frightened by the advances made by the National Democrats" to such an extent that we have turned all our attention to their rivals. But the fact of the matter is that we categorized the N.D. as a tuppenny-ha'penny party that would soon collapse and was not worth taking too much notice of.

And so the news that the National Democrats had split did not cause much in the way of surprise in the *Expo* editorial office. There will now be a period of unrest in the "nationalist" ranks.

A large proportion of those who have left the party in recent weeks are the activists who, for some reason, had got it into their heads that despite everything the N.D. had something to do with "democracy." They complain about the lack of internal party democracy and are horrified by the all-too-obvious traits of Nazism. Many of them are highly likely to find their way back into the Sweden Democrats, once again believing that the S.D. have something to do with "democracy."

The Sweden Democrats have benefited from the breakaway of the National Democrats. It has meant that they could discard a lot of their unwanted ballast in the form of criminals and activists with Nazi links; and now the S.D. are in the advantageous position of being able to pick and choose between the wheat and the chaff of the activists who come crawling back home, cap in hand.

The National Democrats will no doubt survive, and remain as a label in the nationalist movement. But having lost their comparatively house-trained "democrats," the party will appear all the more like a Nazi sect alongside the Svenska Motståndsrörelsen (Swedish Resistance Movement) and similar groups. The presence of such characters as Marc Abramson and Vavra Suk will guarantee that.

Which means that the National Democrats can be put to one side.

Notes

1. Salem is a municipality to the south of Stockholm. In 2000 the small community was shaken by the murder of a young skinhead, Daniel Wretström. The perpetrators had an immigrant background, and the Nazi movement declared the murder proof of an escalating racism against Swedes. Daniel Wretström became a martyr for the movement, and since then a demonstration has been held in Salem to honor his memory.
2. In 2003, National Democratic Youth carried out a violent attack on participants in the Gay Pride Festival in Stockholm. The party's chairman, Marc Abramsson, was subsequently imprisoned for battery and rioting.

AN ATTACK ON DEMOCRACY

www.expo.se
September 11, 2003

At the time of writing we have no idea who murdered Foreign Minister Anna Lindh. It might have been an ideologically motivated incident with some kind of political background, or it might have been the work of a madman. All we know for certain is that the murderer is a cowardly wretch.

Irrespective of the motives behind the murder, it is an attack on democracy and freedom of speech. There is no more definitive attack on freedom of speech than murder.

Comparisons with the murder of Olof Palme are inescapable. Anna Lindh was forty-six when she was murdered.

She began her career as an official in the Social Democratic Youth movement and a colleague of Olof Palme in the 1980s, and was one of the politicians who continued to carry out his legacy.

Anna Lindh was respected as one of the country's best known politicians, generally regarded as a capable one. The respect was not based simply on her political standpoints—people were always for or against, of course—but on her ability to communicate with ordinary people, to listen to what they had to say and to act in a humane and democratic way.

Nevertheless, the attack on Anna Lindh is not surprising. Irrespective of who eventually is identified as her killer, he has acted in a climate in which politicians and public figures are increasingly legitimate targets for crude hate campaigns of various kinds. Olof Palme experienced this unrelenting hatred for many years before he was murdered. And since then politicians from all the democratic parties have been subjected to similar campaigns.

There are groups and individuals who seem to have nothing better to do than to stir up that kind of hatred and distrust of democratic politicians. It is a phenomenon not restricted to the far right, but can be found in several political contexts. Having said that, there is no doubt that racist, Nazi and anti-democratic groups devote themselves to that sort of rumor-spreading and campaigning more than any others.

Such campaigners have been working flat out for the last twenty-four hours. In such circumstances the Internet is the most important weapon of those devoted to the politics of hatred. Hiding behind pseudonyms or anonymity, the most cowardly of the opinionated can churn out their message to their heart's content—it is of course always the case that those responsible for the crudest attacks never show their faces. Typical examples are some of the activists on the simple-minded chat page "*Exilen*" ("The Exile"),[1] which is patronized by Sweden Democrats, National Democrats and Nazis. A few of the contributors display a degree of common sense, but at least as many post anonymous comments drenched in *Schadenfreude* expressing the opinions of people who remain steeped in hatred.

Only an hour after the knife attack on Anna Lindh, somebody signing himself as "M.S." commented: "What a pity that the injuries are not life-threatening." That tells us all we need to know about "M.S."

A few minutes later "Blue-and-Yellow" wrote: "By being a member of our treacherous multi-culti-loving government, which opens the door wide to an invasion of Arabs who rape, rob, murder and assault Swedes [. . .]—She is a rotten apple. She deserves all she gets."

"Fritänkaren" (Freethinker) alleges a conspiratorial angle, suggesting that Göran Persson might be behind the murder and stating that "if the Fat One himself is not behind the attack, perhaps it might be an eye-opener and make him less anti-Swedish in future."

"Doctor Malan" claims that Anna Lindh "is indirectly responsible for the death and suffering of many people" and hopes that "the socialist whore will die!" "Doctor Malan" is of course an ugly customer of the worst order. Unfortunately he and many of those like him are working assiduously to influence the ideology of a lot of young people.

The neo-Nazi online magazine *Info-14* expressed enthusiasm. Shortly after news of the attack broke on Wednesday they posted the headline: "Traitor of the people carved up." And so on.

Today the leader of the Sweden Democrats, Mikael Jansson, regrets the death of Anna Lindh. His party and his colleagues belong to the circle that has consistently stirred up distrust and hatred of the Foreign Minister, not least via their representatives on *"Exilen"* and similar chat pages. As recently as this past summer (July 30, 2003) the deputy leader of the S.D., Björn Söder, wrote an article on the S.D. home page featuring Anna Lindh, with the headline "The Social Democrats invite ex-terrorists." The reference was to Joschka Fischer, Germany's Foreign Minister.

"The party proclaims with pride in a press release that Anna Lindh and Joschka Fischer will take part in an event linked to the Social Democrats' economics seminar."

Shortly after the elections last year (October 22, 2002) the S.D. attacked Anna Lindh because in her capacity as Foreign Minister she had done what her job required and interceded on behalf of a 42-year-old Swedish Iraqi who had been sentenced to a long period of imprisonment in Iraq. The article was written by Felix Svensson (who is well known as a resident of Malmö and one of the Islamophobes on the *"Exilen"* website), and protested about the government using taxpayers' money for this purpose.

Party Secretary Tommy Funebo stirs up contempt for politicians (October 14, 2001) in connection with the attack on the World Trade Center. He dismisses Göran Persson and Anna Lindh as "starry-eyed powers-that-be."

A few days earlier the S.D. website had posted an article claiming that "the government and parliament had partly financed the attack on the World Trade Center."

Funebo reveals the Sweden Democrats' attitude to Anna Lindh and the democratically elected government when (March 31, 2001) he comments on a speech given by Anna Lindh at a conference for human rights in Switzerland. When Lindh demands that all governments must be open to scrutiny with regard to the way in which human rights are protected in any given country, Funebo comments that the Sweden Democrats' "human rights are violated every day by Anna Lindh's Social Democratic government."

The political climate in Sweden will be affected by that attack on Anna Lindh. There is no doubt about that. But the political climate has been changing bit by bit for many years.

Note

1. *"Exilen"* was a chat forum that for a time became the centre of the Swedish xenophobic debate. The forum is no longer active.

the most cowardly of the opinionated can churn out their message to their heart's content—it is of course always the case that those responsible for the crudest attacks never show their faces. Typical examples are some of the activists on the simple-minded chat page "*Exilen*" ("The Exile"),[1] which is patronized by Sweden Democrats, National Democrats and Nazis. A few of the contributors display a degree of common sense, but at least as many post anonymous comments drenched in *Schadenfreude* expressing the opinions of people who remain steeped in hatred.

Only an hour after the knife attack on Anna Lindh, somebody signing himself as "M.S." commented: "What a pity that the injuries are not life-threatening." That tells us all we need to know about "M.S."

A few minutes later "Blue-and-Yellow" wrote: "By being a member of our treacherous multi-culti-loving government, which opens the door wide to an invasion of Arabs who rape, rob, murder and assault Swedes [. . .]—She is a rotten apple. She deserves all she gets."

"Fritänkaren" (Freethinker) alleges a conspiratorial angle, suggesting that Göran Persson might be behind the murder and stating that "if the Fat One himself is not behind the attack, perhaps it might be an eye-opener and make him less anti-Swedish in future."

"Doctor Malan" claims that Anna Lindh "is indirectly responsible for the death and suffering of many people" and hopes that "the socialist whore will die!" "Doctor Malan" is of course an ugly customer of the worst order. Unfortunately he and many of those like him are working assiduously to influence the ideology of a lot of young people.

The neo-Nazi online magazine *Info-14* expressed enthusiasm. Shortly after news of the attack broke on Wednesday they posted the headline: "Traitor of the people carved up."

And so on.

Today the leader of the Sweden Democrats, Mikael Jansson, regrets the death of Anna Lindh. His party and his colleagues belong to the circle that has consistently stirred up distrust and hatred of the Foreign Minister, not least via their representatives on *"Exilen"* and similar chat pages. As recently as this past summer (July 30, 2003) the deputy leader of the S.D., Björn Söder, wrote an article on the S.D. home page featuring Anna Lindh, with the headline "The Social Democrats invite ex-terrorists." The reference was to Joschka Fischer, Germany's Foreign Minister.

"The party proclaims with pride in a press release that Anna Lindh and Joschka Fischer will take part in an event linked to the Social Democrats' economics seminar."

Shortly after the elections last year (October 22, 2002) the S.D. attacked Anna Lindh because in her capacity as Foreign Minister she had done what her job required and interceded on behalf of a 42-year-old Swedish Iraqi who had been sentenced to a long period of imprisonment in Iraq. The article was written by Felix Svensson (who is well known as a resident of Malmö and one of the Islamophobes on the *"Exilen"* website), and protested about the government using taxpayers' money for this purpose.

Party Secretary Tommy Funebo stirs up contempt for politicians (October 14, 2001) in connection with the attack on the World Trade Center. He dismisses Göran Persson and Anna Lindh as "starry-eyed powers-that-be."

DEAR *EXPO* . . .

www.expo.se
September 26, 2003

Dear *Expo*,

Why do you not write anything about the Nazi (aged thirty-five) who was arrested for the murder of Anna Lindh? Hang the swine out to dry. Why the silence on your home page?

"J."

Dear J.,

We don't write anything about the 35-year-old because we don't have anything to say about him. Since he was arrested the telephones here at *Expo* have been red-hot. The most frequent question from the mass media when things have been at their most intense has been to do with what we know about his links with Nazism, which organization he belonged to, etc.

Our answer has been that we cannot confirm that he is a known active Nazi. There is no end to the rumours circulating, placing him in one or other organization—they suggest that he is an active Nazi, a long-standing member of the V.A.M., active in the Nationalist Youth, the National Democrats, the National Socialist Front, and so on.

The only facts that we can confirm are that seventeen years ago he was found guilty of painting a swastika on a wall. He is on the criminal register, but the crimes he committed are not particularly serious, and not of the kind that we usually associate with Nazis.

Apart from that *Expo* has been unable to find any reliable documentation to substantiate the many claims of this kind coming from mainly unknown sources. The 35-year-old has been moving in circles where he has come into contact with Nazis; but, there again, he has also been moving in lots of other circles. Hence *Expo* is unable to verify any of the allegations that have been made, and has no desire to add to the speculations—and so we have written nothing about him.

———

Dear Stieg,

You seem to be able to detect a connection between the way the Sweden Democrats "stir up" hatred and the murder of Anna Lindh. Isn't this a bit far-fetched? If you can point to guilty people other than the actual perpetrator, should you not spell out the alleged connection? It's enough, for example, to look at Peter Eriksson's pronouncement last week in which he denounces all Sweden Democrats as vermin. Talk about stirring up hatred in a way reminiscent of "*Der ewige Jude*" [The Eternal Jew] . . . And then there is the car-bomb attack on the leader of the National Democrats, which was even reported in the established press. Not to mention the Gothenburg riots,[1] when a large number of opinion-formers came forward to defend the violence initiated by masked youths. In my view the cause has more to do with the fact that the likes of you seem to defend political violence so long as it is directed at people with the "wrong" opinions. [...] So instead of immediately accusing the Sweden Democrats of using their rhetoric to stir up violence, you should distance yourself from ALL political violence, whether it is aimed at Social Democrats or Sweden Democrats.

"Anonymous"

Dear Anonymous.

Thank you for your message. The day after the murder of Anna Lindh I wrote a leader on *Expo*'s home page about the circumstances in which politicians have to operate. Needless to say, I did not suggest that the knife had been held by the hand of a Sweden Democrat.

My text was about hate campaigns that create a climate in which it is legitimate to hate public figures, and which obviously helps to create a mentality that leads to murder. I identified a few sources of that kind of hate campaign, and quoted from some of the commentaries that had already been posted on the Internet even before Anna Lindh was killed. Are you suggesting we should pretend that kind of rhetoric doesn't exist?

I wrote specifically that "Irrespective of who is eventually identified as the murderer, he has acted in an increasingly implacable political climate in which politicians and public figures are legitimate targets for crude hate campaigners of various kinds." Which is something quite different from what you read into my article. But you think that the reasoning is far-fetched. I don't.

And then you argue that people like me defend violence as long as it is directed at people with the "wrong" views. You mention the Gothenburg riots and the bomb attack on the car of a far-right extremist.

Where on earth have you got that rubbish from? *Expo* explicitly denounces all violence, and I defy you to find a single quotation from our web pages to justify your accusation. Of course we think it is disgraceful that people are exposed to politically motivated violence, regardless of the individual target. Having said that, *Expo* specializes in keeping an eye on the extreme right. A number of attacks on right-wing extremists does not excuse for one moment the far-right hate campaigns that have been waged for many years against leading politicians, and the extreme right cannot hide behind some excuse to the effect that they are merely getting their own back.

———

Stieg Larsson,

Having read your article on expo.se, I find that your name is etched upon my cornea. [. . .] You fumbled to summon up your anti-Swedish conscience and concocted what you yourself usually call conspiracy theories. Do I have to remind you where a large part of contemporary political violence comes from, and where the real anti-democratic forces are based? Yes, from people like you who, in your articles, often defend the N.M.R., A.F.A. and other left-wing sects.[2] [. . .] Take Salem, for instance: you are only too pleased to defend the sects that assaulted a family with young children, injured police officers, and disturbed the peace on a day that was devoted to grief.

"Viktor"

Dear Viktor,

Expo has never—in no circumstance and not even in passing or indirectly—defended anyone who has assaulted a family with young children, injured police officers or horses, nor (come to that) the murder of the central character, Daniel Wretström. If you have evidence to the contrary, please produce without delay quotations, text or video clips. At several hundred public meetings I have always distanced myself from violence.

Expo was the first public institution in Sweden to distance itself from what happened in Salem, thanks to Kurdo Baksi, in the most devastating wording possible the day after the murder. Kurdo wrote to the effect that it was disgusting that a seventeen-year-old lad, no matter who he was, should not be able to wait at a bus stop without risk of being stabbed to death.

———

Dear *Expo*,

What do you have to say to this, then? You must be feeling bitter,
Stieg. Let's face it, Anna Lindh's murderer wasn't after all a far-right
extremistswedennationalistmadmannazi, but a Yugoslavian citizen,
and moreover the victim of humiliation in a psychological ward—
the kind of treatment the government you are all in favour of put in
place. Tough, Stieg, tough.

Message to *"Exilen"* from "Anonymous"

Dear Anonymous,

The hand that wielded the knife isn't of interest. What is bitter and
tough to accept in this deplorable incident is that Sweden has lost
an excellent politician and Foreign Minister.

What my article was about was that certain groups encourage
contempt of politicians and encourage a climate for debates which
suggest that violence and hate campaigns are legitimate. The fact
that Anna Lindh's murderer was of Yugoslavian extraction has
no bearing on that fact. But what is regrettable is that the usual
collection of xenophobic groups will have an excuse to exploit the
murder in order to create unrest in society.

The National Democrats, with ill-concealed *Schadenfreude*,
have already pointed out on their website that the accused is a
second-generation immigrant from Yugoslavia. The N.D. goes on
to claim that:

> Anna Lindh's life-work was devoted to abolishing Swedish
> borders, to deconstructing the Swedish welfare state and
> to ensuring that the Swedish people would lose control of
> their own country as a result of mass immigration. [. . .]
> But in the end the Social Democratic state based on vio-
> lence caught up with her. [. . .] It can be concluded that
> not only did she become a victim of the easy-going Social
> Democratic policy of releasing mentally ill patients from

hospitals, but she also became a victim of her own mass immigration policies.

What exactly are you proposing? That the policy of internal E.U. immigration should also be abolished? Or what? If so, the N.D. can no doubt start by sending home the second-generation Czech who has been operating as one of the party's main ideological policy-makers.[3]

Notes

1. The Gothenburg riots coincided with U.S. President George Bush's visit to the city between June 14 and 16, 2001. A total of around fifty police officers and ninety demonstrators were injured.
2. N.M.R. (the Network Against Racism), and A.F.A. (Anti-Fascist Action), are both militant anti-fascist groups. N.M.R. was formed in the second half of the '90s as a cooperative organization for anti-racist groups. A.F.A. was founded in 1993 and is made up of an international network of similar groups across Europe. The group has several times been responsible for violent attacks on political opponents.
3. National Democrat ideologue Vavra Suk is from a Czech family. The family fled communist oppression and found a safe haven in Sweden.

THE INTELLECTUAL BREAKDOWN OF *EXPRESSEN*

www.expo.se
September 5, 2003

The E.M.U. debate seems to be more than just a referendum on the Swedish currency. One would presumably have to go as far back as the referendum on nuclear power to find a comparable campaign in which so many intellectually dishonest arguments have been floated in such a short time.

In recent weeks the "No" camp has repeatedly been castigated—and rightly so—for overdramatizing and scaremongering and using dishonest arguments of no relevance. "Is it not Hitler who is really behind the E.U.?" asked Sweden's highest-circulation evening tabloid, *Expressen*, among others.

But as voting day approaches the "Yes" camp is lagging behind in the opinion polls. Now every trick in the book has suddenly become permissible. It is no longer a question of producing factual arguments for or against the E.M.U.; it is a matter of smears and innuendo accusing opponents of hidden intentions.

Expressen's new correspondent is Johan Rinderheim, the "chief ideologue" of the Sweden Democrats and a local councilor in Nynäshamn. In what must be regarded as the year's biggest political flop, the opinion editors have invited him to smear Centre Party leader Maud Olofsson with the putrefied rubbish that oozes out of the far right.

Not surprisingly Olofsson is upset and feels that she has been portrayed as a right-wing extremist. She has every reason to feel aggrieved. The point of Rinderheim's article is to show that she and the Centre somehow support the chauvinistic nationalistic attitudes of Rinderheim's own party. This is not the case, of course, as *Expressen*'s editors are well aware.

The Sweden Democrats are a racist and anti-democratic party that believes in conspiracy theories. The Centre is a democratic party with a tradition of excluding racists, anti-democrats and conspiracy theorists. As recently as a few months ago the party expelled a local councilor in Skövde who failed to meet the required standards of democracy.

The fact that the Sweden Democrats are against the E.M.U. and above all the E.U. is not so remarkable or surprising. The party has chauvinistic isolationist policies in which the E.U. is regarded as a threat quite simply because it opens the doors for a flexible labor market, and hence there is a risk that various dark-haired and brown-eyed people might sneak into the country. According to the Sweden Democrats' propaganda, dark-haired and brown-eyed people are prone to have criminal records and to commit gang rape. And so the party is against the E.U. All that is understandable.

But that makes it the more difficult to fathom why, in the last frantic days before the referendum, *Expressen* chooses to open the doors to the kind of debating technique one might expect to find emanating from anti-democratic parties such as the Sweden Democrats. One is tempted to agree with *Falu-Kuriren*'s pithy leading article.[1] Shame on you.

In order to give some kind of intellectual legitimacy to the choice of Johan Rinderheim as a correspondent, *Expressen* maintains that it is "relevant" to scrutinize the views of the Sweden Democrats on the E.M.U. question, hence also Maud Olofsson's links with the extreme right. It is even claimed on their leader page that publishing Rinderheim's article can be seen as part of *Expressen*'s rejection of racism and intolerance. The question this raises is how the publication of Sweden Democratic propaganda without comment can be said to be "scrutiny" or "rejection." It is sheer nonsense, of course.

Even more remarkable is the justification when a spokesman for *Expressen* maintains that Maud Olofsson herself has chosen to join political forces with the Sweden Democrats and (in Thursday's *Expressen*) also the National Socialist Front.

Using exactly the same debating technique, it is easy to demonstrate that *Expressen* and the "Yes" campaign have chosen to align themselves with Morgens Glistrup, who is after all a warm supporter of the E.U. Or why not Hell's Angels and various gangster syndicates, who have nothing against a common currency being introduced throughout Europe since it would make it easier to launder money made from drugs? It is not difficult to pick out ten points on which the wording in the S.D.'s party program is in accordance with key questions on *Expressen*'s leader page. Should we therefore draw the conclusion that there is something fishy about *Expressen*'s political views because their values are shared by right-wing extremists?

Most remarkable, however, is that in the course of discussions the next day *Expressen* does not seem to realize that it has made an intellectual blunder of almost cosmic proportions. By choosing the Sweden Democrats as their partner with the aim of smearing Maud Olofsson, the newspaper has introduced a new political equation into Sweden.

First, *Expressen* has established that arguments made by the Sweden Democrats have the same impeccable legitimacy and intellectual value as those made by normal democratic parties. This is the very point of printing the article by Johan Rinderheim without critical comment—no doubt he chuckled all the way back to his party headquarters after achieving the biggest propaganda success since he launched the campaign of violence at the end of the 1990s. The fact that the very next day Rinderheim distanced himself from any suggestion of support for Maud Olofsson on the S.D. website is consistent. His hope is that Centre Party voters will be tempted to regard the S.D. as a political alternative, and to that end he has now received public support from *Expressen* in a way that cannot be gauged in financial terms.

The Sweden Democrats have thus achieved an aim for which the party has striven since its predecessors were marching around in uniforms dragging their knuckles on the ground: the Swedish media will present the party just like any normal democratic party you care to name.

In that vein *Expressen* has established that there is no difference between the Sweden Democrats and the Centre Party. That means that in the next election campaign either the Centre Party must be excluded from non-socialist cooperation, or all the non-socialist parties must make a joint declaration that it is permitted to cooperate with the Sweden Democrats.

Expressen was thus the first newspaper in Sweden to give in to the temptation that their media colleagues in Austria and other countries have previously fallen for—and bitterly regretted: the belief that the nationalist movement can be exploited for personal political interests. A typical example was when Mitterrand tried to use Le Pen in order to split non-socialist voters in France. The only effect was that support for Le Pen grew to 10 percent.

All that *Expressen*'s campaign-makers can now do is to go back to school as soon as possible. They could start by making a study visit to editors Lindqvist on *Falu-Kuriren* and Koskinen on *Norrtelje Tidning*.[2] They are not afraid to publish letters to the editor from the far right, but they scrutinize the arguments expressed and answer them in detail—they do not allow themselves to be used as a megaphone for their own political interests. That is what democrats do.

Notes

1. *Falu-Kuriren* is an independent local liberal daily newspaper based in the Swedish province of Dalarna.
2. *Norrtelje Tidning* is published five days a week in Norrtälje municipality, north of Stockholm. The magazine was owned by the Centre Party, but then sold to the media company Promedia.

THE PEA-BRAINS OF NATIONALISM

www.expo.se
January 26, 2004

In many respects the National Democrats (N.D.) are the pea-brains of Swedish nationalism. The party was founded as a breakaway faction of the Sweden Democrats (S.D.) in 2001. Since the mid-1990s the S.D.'s strategy had been to distance themselves from uniformed Nazism because too many uniforms meant reduced credibility in the polling booths.

The N.D. came into being as a protest against the S.D. having become too "liberalized." The defectors took with them a number of activists, mainly from the S.D.'s youth branch. In formal party propaganda and press releases the

N.D. present themselves as a "democratic party." In fact they are an anti-democratic nationalist group of madmen that believe in conspiracy theories and are closely linked to Nazism. Behind the façade party members discuss anti-Jewish conspiracy theories and officially conduct crude hate campaigns against homosexuals and Muslims. Politicians who do not agree with the National Democrats are routinely branded as left-wing extremists or traitors, irrespective of the party they belong to. A large number of N.D. members who have joined over the last two years have come from nationalist sects such as Nationell Ungdom (National Youth).[1] The party is therefore well integrated with the Nazi movement, from which it takes its ideological framework.

The N.D. toss the word "democracy" around on public occasions, but at the same time proclaim Nazi propaganda at meetings for members—in other words, they are Nazis with a pseudo-democratic façade.

It is not difficult to find examples. N.D. were one of the main organizers of the Nazi Salem March last December, with their informal leader Tor Paulsson as speaker. He was accompanied by the likes of Anders Ärleskog, leader of the National Socialist Front, "Pastor" Magnus Söderman, one of the leaders of the Svenska Motståndsrörelsen (Swedish Resistance Movement), and Thomas Ölund from Blood and Honour. That is the company the National Democrats keep.

In his speech Tor Paulsson promised that democratic politicians "will be punished."

"One day all those who have contributed to oppression, violations and humiliations will receive their just punishment. Gudrun Schyman,[2] Göran Persson and all the other traitors will have to answer for what they have done to us. I promise you all: that punishment will strike home," Tor Paulsson said.

That is National Democratic rhetoric—in other words, nothing that can be mistaken for a democratic view of reality.

It was the Nationaldemokraternas Ungdomsförbund (N.D.U.—National Democratic Youth Association), its leader Marc Abramsson and a selection of activists from neo-Nazi organizations that attacked the Pride Festival last summer and badly injured Facundo Unia.

As the Pride procession was taking place in Stockholm, a hundred or so Nazis and N.D.U. activists gathered on Slottsbacken to hold a counter-demonstration under the banner "Crush the gay lobby." They started some distance away from the procession, but then came closer and closer to the parade on Skeppsbron. Not surprisingly, bottles began to be thrown and people were assaulted. A child in a pram was hit by glass splinters.

There is no question about it being the Nazis who attacked the Pride procession. There is no other explanation of the fact that the N.D.U. gang assembled on Slottsbacken and then closed in on the parade. Some of those taking part were assaulted in front of cameras and witnesses. The person most badly injured was Facundo Unia. He tried to run away but stumbled and was surrounded by up to ten Nazis, who pummeled him with kicks and punches and blows with sticks. Battered and covered in blood, he was taken by ambulance to the Söder hospital. Thirty-nine members of the party and the party's youth branch and several well-known Nazis were taken into custody in connection with the attack.

In the subsequent rhetoric the National Democrats maintained that it was in fact the Pride marchers who attacked the N.D.U. This claim is so absurd that even the most loyal N.D. supporter could not possibly believe it.

As rhetorical lies are the main weapon in the National Democrats' propaganda arsenal, we shall no doubt be treated to more such bunkum in the near future. The nationalist pea-brains have since then attacked two journalists, *Expo* staff Daniel Poohl and Daniel Olsson, who were doing their job and covering a public meeting arranged by the N.D. in Gothenburg last Saturday.

Poohl and Olsson are relatively used to being exposed to threats, jostling and gobs of spittle. It goes with the territory, as it were. But on this occasion they reported to the police a named local N.D. leader. The *Expo* editorial office supports that action 100 percent.

On their home page the National Democrats describe their rally as "successful." They claim that while marching away from the square after the meeting, a handful of "left-wing extremists" and "badly organized anarchistic anti-democrats" turned up and tried to provoke trouble. However, the N.D. security guards were able to disperse them with no problem, according to the home page.

So as far as the National Democrats are concerned, "no problem" covers a young woman beaten up; two party activists arrested, one of them carrying a knife; a candidate for the Mölndal local council reported for assault; two journalists attacked, as well as a large number of Gothenburg residents scared stiff. Such a list would no doubt be regarded as a problem by a democratic party.

The National Democrats held their meeting in the square called Harry Hjörnes Plats. They say themselves that the location was not coincidental, but chosen for symbolical reasons as part of their protest about the mass media.

The journalist Harry Hjörne became editor of the local newspaper *Göteborgs-Posten* in 1926 and turned it into one of Sweden's most important dailies. In the universe inhabited by the National Democrats, *Göteborgs-Posten* is a treasonable publication—"a newspaper that never misses an opportunity to oppose the interests of the Swedish people, and which has made several untruthful allegations about the National Democrats."

The National Democrats disapprove of the democratic mass media, which tend not to publish N.D. propaganda.

Regarding journalists as a treasonable threat is an attitude that has persisted ever since the National Democrats were founded in the August of 2001. The location was Brygghuset in Stockholm.

Three journalists were present: Mikael Ekman from *Expo* and Johan Ander and Henrik Hansson from *Expressen*. They were stopped in the entrance hall. When they asked to speak to somebody in authority, a furious Tor Paulsson came rushing out and accused them of being "bloody terrorists," and said that if the journalists didn't go away within ten seconds he would "assist" their departure.

The National Democrats' security guards escorted the journalists until they were over four hundred meters away from the hall. That is not how democrats act.

Notes

1. Nationell Ungdom was formed in the mid-1990s and in 2006 was merged with the youth branch of the Nazi organization Svenska Motståndrörelsen (Swedish Resistance Movement).
2. Gudrun Schyman is a Swedish politician who served as leader of the Swedish Left Party from 1993 to 2003 and remained a member of the party until 2004, when she left to focus on her political work in the party's feminist initiative.

"THE WORLD'S MOST DANGEROUS PROFESSION"

From *Överleva deadline: handbook för hotade journalister*
(Surviving the Deadlines: A Handbook for Threatened
Journalists), Svenska Journalistförbundet, 2000

What do you do if you are attacked by Nazis?—Run like hell.

This was the off-the-cuff response by the English journalist Graeme Atkinson, European editor for the past twenty years of the journal *Searchlight*, which has specialized in infiltrating and exposing far-right extremist groups involved in violent and terrorist activities.

Searchlight has identified anti-Semites who defiled synagogues, exposed plans for a bomb attack on the Notting Hill Carnival, spelled out links between European terrorist networks and illegal arms deals involving Northern

Ireland, and in recent years focused on the black economy surrounding "white-power music."

Graeme Atkinson has more than enough experience of being exposed to the threat of right-wing extremist violence. He is one of the ten or twelve journalists in Europe who have received more death threats than any others. In the 1970s he was badly beaten up and had his nose broken by Nazis. On at least two occasions serious plans to assault him have been uncovered and thwarted in time.

For the last fifteen years he has been forced to live in virtual anonymity. Only a few of his friends and colleagues know his real home address. Hardly any outsiders even know in which European country he currently lives.

Guarding his personal safety is a way of life imposed upon Atkinson by necessity.

In the days leading up to November 30, 1989, he was commissioned by the B.B.C. program "Panorama" to guide a young television presenter through the neo-Nazi labyrinths of Europe. They travelled to Stockholm, and for security reasons Atkinson used an assumed name. Nevertheless, the fact that he was taking part in the B.B.C. project had leaked out and a reception committee of over thirty skinheads awaited him outside Fryshuset.

When a Swedish journalist later interrogated the skinheads, they replied surprisingly frankly in front of a television camera that the mission they had been tasked with was to "kick him to bits." Someone had faxed to them a photograph and a description of Atkinson. At the same time somebody had issued instructions to the effect that the B.B.C. presenter was not to be touched. In other words, Atkinson was specifically picked out as a target for assault.

It was pure chance that Atkinson was saved. The skinheads expected him to arrive with a lone B.B.C. reporter, when they would have had no problem in identifying him. In fact seven people turned up, including a cameraman recruited from Swedish television, sound technicians, drivers and a Swedish journalist who had been assisting those involved with background material. In the confusion that ensued, Atkinson smelled a rat and at the last moment managed to beat a retreat. Had he not done so, it would have been odds-on him being another headline in the evening newspapers.

Graeme Atkinson is admittedly an extreme case of a journalist forced by motives of sheer self-preservation to adapt his everyday life to accommodate security routines that to outsiders could well be deemed half-paranoid. But he is by no means alone.

The International Federation of Journalists (I.F.J.), which regularly monitors the freedom of the press and working conditions of journalists all over the world, maintains solemnly that to be a journalist is one of the world's most dangerous professions. Statistics from the I.F.J. show that in the 1990s at least 662 journalists or media workers were killed in the course of their duties. The statistics for the 1990s are as follows:

Year	Number of journalists killed*
1990	46
1991	84
1992	66
1993	75
1994	114
1995	65
1996	47
1997	47
1998	31
1999	87
Total	1662

(* The statistics include all media workers: journalists, photographers, sound technicians, producers etc.)

Another hundred or so deaths of journalists who met a violent death can be added to those statistics, deaths that are still being investigated by the I.F.J., and where it is not yet clear whether they were directly linked to the work being undertaken.

The statistics cover murder, "disappearance," deaths connected to the coverage of war or similar events, and pure accidents that happened to occur while the journalist was working.

There is no sign of any improvement in the statistics so far available for 2000. The I.F.J. notes that by May this year at least twenty-six journalists or other media workers have been killed. Any reader who wishes to find out more about particular cases can visit the I.F.J.'s home page on www.ifj.org.

In the 1990s well-known hotbeds of conflicts were responsible for a large proportion of the deaths. According to the I.F.J., the unusually high death rate in 1994 is explained by the fact that many journalists died in connection with the civil wars in the former Yugoslavia and Rwanda. Other hotbeds of conflict were Algeria, Indonesia, Chechnya and Georgia.

The statistics indicate that the profession of journalism is especially dangerous in certain countries. During the 1990s at least thirty-three journalists were killed in Russia, many of them murdered or targeted for assault. A lot of these cases are still unresolved.

In Colombia, where the Medellin cartel and death squadrons operate, the statistics are especially horrific. Forty-eight journalists were killed in Colombia—over 7 percent of the total number killed in the last decade. A large proportion of these deaths were assassinations or contract killings with political or criminal affiliations.

A typical example from Colombia is the murder of the television journalist Jaime Garzón, who was shot by two masked men on motorcycles on August 13, 1999. Garzón, who was a political commentator on Caracol Television, was a well-known supporter of the peace process, and on several occasions had urged the government in Bogotá to open negotiations with the country's left-wing guerrillas.

His political message gave rise to a series of threats. One of those threatening Garzón during the weeks before his death was Carlos Castaño, leader of the far-right paramilitary group Auto-defensa Unidas de Colombia (A.U.C.), which is thought to be behind a large proportion of violent deaths in the country.

In a press release only a few hours after the murder, the A.U.C. claimed responsibility. Like so many other political murders in Colombia, the case of Jaime Garzón is yet to be solved.

The I.F.J.'s statistics also suggest that Graeme Atkinson and his colleagues on *Searchlight* have good reason to take their personal safety very seriously. The combination of investigative journalism, political extremism and criminality has a tendency to lead to threats.

This can be illustrated by a few international instances from the 1990s:

In 1993 Giuseppe Alfano, aged forty-two, was murdered on the road between Palermo and Messina on the north coast of Sicily. He was killed by a single bullet in the head. The murder is still unsolved. Alfano worked for the newspaper *La Sicilia* and was regarded as a specialist in exposing the mafia and its links with both right-wing extremism and local political groups.

In 1996 Bernard Gautier, aged thirty-five, was found hanged on the holiday island of Menorca. Gautier was the Spain correspondent of the French newspaper *Le Figaro*. The police investigation concluded that the death was a case of suicide, which is strongly disputed by Gautier's family. Not only was Gautier tied up, he also had a blue cross painted on his shirt, and the word "traitor" had been daubed on the wall. At the time of his death he was investigating illegal arms trading in connection with the war in Bosnia.

One of the decade's most discussed murders of a journalist took place in 1996 in Ireland. The victim was Veronica Guerin, aged thirty-six and a crime reporter for the *Sunday Independent*. Guerin had stopped for a red traffic light in central Dublin when two men on a motorcycle rode up and shot her five times. Guerin specialized in corruption and organized crime linked with drug dealing. She had received several death threats before the murder.

In 1999 Oleg Chervonyuk, aged thirty-seven and an editor on *Novosti Press* in St. Petersburg, was shot and killed outside his home. The murder is still unsolved. The police investigation suggests it was a contract killing linked to the Russian mafia.

Obviously, journalists in countries ruled by traditional dictatorships are at greater risk than their colleagues in democratic countries. In such states there is a tendency for journalists to "commit suicide" when they are arrested by the police.

The situation can be illustrated by the case of Sayfeddin Tepe, aged twenty-seven and the correspondent of the newspaper *Yeni Politika* in Turkey. In 1995 Tepe and two other journalists were arrested by the police. Tepe's colleagues were released more or less straight away, but Tepe was taken to the interrogation center in the prison at Bitlis. About a week after his arrest it was announced by the local authorities that Tepe had "committed suicide by hanging himself in his underclothes."

Tepe's family have objected vehemently to this explanation, and a post-mortem showed that he had been subjected to extreme torture before his death. It should be mentioned that Sayfeddin Tepe's cousin Ferhat Tepe—also a journalist—had died in similar murky circumstances two years previously.

In these respects, and in many others, Sweden has been spared the sort of political or criminal violence that has affected our international colleagues: but even here things have become noticeably more hazardous in recent years.

As is well known, in 1999 a Swedish journalist came very close to becoming one of the I.F.J. statistics when the free-lance reporters Peter Karlsson and Katarina Larsson were victims of a car bombing in Nacka.

It was Karlsson and his eight-year-old son who were affected. On the morning of June 27, Peter prepared to drive his son to a playground. The family car had been parked outside their home during the night, and when he started the engine he detonated a powerful explosive device under-neath the car.

According to the police investigation, the bomb was designed to kill—yet miraculously, both passengers sur-vived. However, Peter suffered very severe spinal injuries, and has needed to undergo several operations. A year after the bomb attack he is still suffering from the after-effects.

For several months before the car-bombing Karlsson and Larsson were subjected to threats. As freelancers for several news-papers including *Aftonbladet*, they had spe-cialized in investigative journalism involving the so-called white-power industry—the production of racist hate pro-paganda. White-power music has a turnover of vast annual sums, and in the 1990s has become the most important and most lucrative source of income for neo-Nazism.

One of the results of the reporting by Karlsson and Larsson has been that several international producers of C.D.s refuse to be involved in white-power music, which causes the industry serious financial losses. Just how great the financial damage has been is difficult to assess—the white-power industry depends to a large extent on black-market money.

One year on, nobody has been arrested or even designated a suspect for the car bomb attack. For obvious reasons the police investigation has concentrated on neo-Nazis with links to the circle that in October last year were behind the murder of the syndicalist Björn Söderberg in Sätra.

The police are investigating the three Nazis who were charged with the Söderberg murder in connection with the Nacka bomb. Irrespective of whether anyone is arrested for it, the atrocity means that a new situation has arisen for journalists in Sweden. The Nacka bomb is a watershed which puts Sweden on the same level as Jaime Garzón's Colombia and Veronica Guerin's Ireland and other countries in which gangsters and anti-democratic forces conduct their press policy by threatening or murdering journalists who put them on the spot.

Alongside physical violence there are other means available to render awkward journalists harmless. Over the years far-right groups, not least in England, have become adept at mud-slinging and undermining their political opponents in the mass media. These methods are now starting to appear in Sweden.

The day after the car bomb exploded, the Nazi magazine *Folktribunen* (the People's Tribune) published on its website an article obviously intended to smear Karlsson and Larsson and to distract attention from far-right groups. *Folktribunen* is the organ of Nationell Ungdom/Svenska Motståndsrörelsen (the National Youth/Swedish Resistance Movement), the organization with which Söderberg's murderer has connections. The text, a mish-mash of facts mixed with half-truths and direct lies, maintains that Karlsson "is not the innocent journalist you might think if you only listen to the media's version."

The article goes on to describe him as follows:

> In patriotic circles he is well known as one of the leaders of the violent organization A.F.A. [Anti-Fascist Action]. Peter Karlsson's involvement with this group is well documented. [. . .] Over several years he has compiled a very comprehensive list of Swedes with opinions different from his own. He is well-known to the police passport division for ordering hundreds of passport photographs of Swedish patriots.
>
> These passports together with detailed personal information have been the basis for journalistic attacks on hundreds or perhaps more people all over the country. The most serious aspect is that this material has then been passed on to the violent organization A.F.A., which has used it to make violent attacks on Swedish patriots.

At the same time as this and similar articles were posted on the Internet by the group that the police investigation then had even more reason to look into, a number of people started telephoning various editorial offices in Stockholm with similar messages.

At Tidningarnas Telegrambyrå (the Swedish Central News Agency) I myself received a call suggesting that Peter Karlsson is "an agent of the A.F.A.," and that the car bomb attack was connected with some sort of "internal dispute." A journalist on a national evening paper had a similar call tipping him off that Karlsson was involved in criminal activities and that the car bomb in fact represented "a show-down in the underworld" or possibly "revenge for criminal activities."

In addition to the promulgation of such tips, various people began posting imaginative revelations on "Passagen"[1] and other chat pages on the Internet. One of these said: "It is not necessarily 'neo-Nazis' behind the car-bombing in Nacka. It could also be the A.F.A.! Or some similar organization." A posting on "Passagen" also expounded the theory that the evening newspaper *Aftonbladet* was behind the bombing. "You should NOT be surprised to find that *Aftonbladet* is behind the bomb-ing! After all, we know that *Aftonbladet* publishes a spe-cial kind of journalism based on 'earning money' from the activities of today's national socialists."

So many similar tips and rumors were forthcoming that there are grounds for suspecting that they were part of an organized campaign.

It is not difficult to imagine the aim of such a campaign: the rumors served partly to smear Peter Karlsson and create doubt about his integrity, partly to cause confusion about who carried out the atrocity, and partly to divert attention away from the neo-Nazi groups that had been threatening the pair of journalists for quite some time.

It is hard to say to what extent the cascade of rumors achieved the desired effect. Judging by the number of telephone calls from journalists to *Expo* magazine—Peter Karlsson and Katarina Larsson used to work for *Expo*—some of the rumors were quite effective.

Far and away the most frequent question on days three and four after the bombing was whether *Expo* could confirm that Karlsson was "a leader of A.F.A." or had a serious criminal record. *Expo* was unable to confirm anything of the sort for the simple reason that the allegations were untrue. The "serious criminal record" Peter was accused of having was in fact restricted to having become caught up twice in the early 1990s in violence linked with anti-racist demonstrations. He was fined and given a suspended prison sentence, and subsequently steered well clear of demonstrations.

Most of the Swedish media evidently realized that the rumors were untrue, and in many respects preposterous. The only exception was one morning paper which basically reproduced all the Internet propaganda. As Peter Karlsson spent six hours that day in the operating theatre, it was left to his partner, Katarina Larsson, to reject the accusations. She did so thoroughly. They are not and have never been activists in the A.F.A.

The fact that Nazi propaganda leads to the spreading of rumors that have an impact in the serious mass media is demonstrated by an example from last summer.

A year after the Nacka bomb, an article in one of our biggest provincial newspapers stated as fact that Peter Karlsson had also been found guilty of arson. The writer claimed he had obtained the information from "a reliable source," and hence he was able to expose the truth. There was only one snag: the claim was totally untrue.

The phenomenon of journalists who have become known as opponents of anti-democratic occurrences being subjected to the spreading of false rumors has become increasingly common in Sweden since the beginning of the 1980s. As the number of racist and far-right organizations has increased, so has the number of cases of threats, telephone terror and letter campaigns. Among the well-known targets over the years are the journalists Ingrid Segerstedt-Wiberg, Göran Rosenberg, Larsolof Giertta and Anna-Lena Lodenius, the television entertainer Hagge Geigert, authors such as Per Ahlmark, and others.

The objective is the same, whether the method is being used in Sweden or Colombia: by means of violence or the threat of violence to suppress free speech and scare journalists into silence—to teach the mass media that criticizing certain developments in society leads to uncomfortable problems.

Note

1. A Swedish chat forum.

GANG RAPE AS RACIST PROPAGANDA

www.expo.se
April 16, 2003

The brutal rape of a fourteen-year-old girl in Rissne has become a racist weapon in the Sweden Democrats' propaganda.[1] The S.D. have posted several outpourings on the subject on their home page, and also distributed leaflets in the school in Rissne the girl attended. The leaflet had the headline: "No more rapes—no more multiculture."

It is worthy of note that the Sweden Democrats are not protesting about a girl being raped, but about a Swedish girl being raped by a gang of immigrant boys aged about fifteen or sixteen. They suggest that the rape is a result of our multicultural society.

In an article on the Sweden Democrats' home page, Anders Steen—an S.D. councilor in Haninge—demands that the teenaged rapists "should be deported immediately to the country they came from."

This demand is associated with a number of problems. The youths actually come from Sweden. They were born and grew up in Sweden. They are Swedish citizens. They are Swedes—nothing else. Deporting them "to the country they came from" thus means in this case that they should be deported to Sweden.

It is of course disgraceful that Swedish youths should do such a thing. Just as, to quote Kurdo Baksi, some Kurdish men who recently murdered a nineteen-year-old girl in an "honor killing" bring disgrace down upon Kurdistan. But the perpetrators should be subjected to Swedish justice— not to a Sweden Democratic lynch mob.

Councillor Anders Steen also brings disgrace down upon Sweden. He is exploiting a brutal rape for his own purposes, so that he can preach racist propaganda. When Anders Steen demands that "they should be deported immediately to the country they came from," what he means is that "they should be deported to the country their parents or possibly their grandparents came from." What he is really saying is that because of their cultural background, they are unusually liable to commit gang rape—that such activities are a part of their cultural heritage.

Anders Steen believes that brutal gang rape of this kind has something to do with immigration or with the cultural background of immigrants. He claims that the image of women that these teenaged rapists have is "something unknown in Sweden before mass immigration began."

This means that the local councilor does not have the slightest idea about why women are raped—and even less of an idea about how the problem should be tackled.

Anders Steen has a simple solution: people who commit such crimes, he writes, "have forfeited once and for all their right to live in Sweden." What he is actually saying is that Swedes with dark-colored hair should be deported.

In any case, Steen does not distinguish between the sexes on this point. He wants to throw out immigrant girls as well. He maintains that immigrant girls defend group rape by claiming that Swedish girls should "blame themselves" because they give the impression of offering themselves on a plate.

It is no doubt true that many immigrant girls—and Swedish girls as well—need to undergo a basic course in feminism; but what Anders Steen is trying to impress upon us is that Swedish girls with an immigrant background defend the right of immigrant boys to commit gang rape.

A few years ago Sweden was horrified by an unusually brutal gang rape of a young girl at a camping site in Norrbotten. The girl was so brutally treated that she was hovering on death's door for a long time. She was Swedish. The rapists were blue-eyed and blond-haired Swedes. With the possible exception of a youth from Tornedalen who was of Finnish stock. Where should they be deported to?

Rape has nothing to do with immigrant background. The fact is that some men are violent towards women. They might be Swedes, or Finns, or Chinese. They might be

Christians, Muslims or Jews. They might be on the left or the right of the political spectrum.

But it is only the Sweden Democrats who try to create racism out of the ill-treatment of women.

Note

1. On January 28, 2000, a 14-year-old girl was brutally raped by a gang of youths at Rissne underground station, in northern Stockholm. The rape was widely reported in the media.

EXIT PAULSSON

www.expo.se
June 30, 2004

If the context were not so serious, it would be easy today to write a jokey article about Tor Paulsson. The big shot of the National Democrats and their party organizer was arrested at Midsummer for an exceptionally serious assault on his partner.

Expo does not normally comment on family tragedies. But in this case the context is such that it is more or less impossible not to do so. Tor Paulsson is a public figure—a politician who seeks the support of the general public, who travels the length and breadth of the country preaching the message that treating women violently is something immigrants do, and who a mere two weeks ago appeared on posters all over Sweden as the first name on the N.D.'s list of candidates in the E.U. elections.

Tor Paulsson's partner is also a public figure. She used to be a member of the Sweden Democrats, but has worked for the National Democrats since the party was launched in 2001. Among other things she has stood as a candidate in general elections and has featured in the party's pamphlets, portrayed as the girl at risk of ill-treatment by immigrant men.

Two important points must be made at this stage.

The first is that her political convictions have nothing at all to do with the fact that she has been assaulted. Violence towards women has to do with men's need to control women, and nothing to do with culture. Even if the National Democrats usually claim the opposite, her ill-treatment has nothing to do with the color of her skin or her ethnicity. She is a woman whose life has been transformed into the same catastrophic mess as that of so many other women who have been treated violently by men. In this respect, she deserves the support and sympathy of those around her, and redress for the outrage that has been inflicted upon her.

The second is that what Tor Paulsson has done must have political consequences. The credibility of the National Democrats' message must have reached rock bottom the moment Tor Paulsson raised his fist against his partner.

The Swedish far right has been trumpeting for years that the violent treatment of women is something immigrants do—not real Swedish men. The person who has preached this gospel more than anybody else is Tor Paulsson. He it was who, as a member of the Sweden Democrats, together

with their then chief ideologue, Johan Rinderheim, produced the slogan: "Stop group rape—stop immigration."
This came about in connection with the Rissne debate of
2000, when a teenage girl was the victim of a group rape by
five immigrant youths.

For the nationalist movement, this message is one of the
most important components of their anti-immigrant propaganda. It has nothing to do with safeguarding women's
rights, but is an attack on an ethnic group. The National
Democrats are a racist party. Their bread and butter is stirring up distrust and hatred of immigrants. Emotionally
describing specific male immigrants as potential rapists is
thus a part of their propaganda.

That is why the National Democrats, the Sweden Democrats, the National Socialist Front, National Youth, Info-14
and other "nationalistic" groups fill their home pages with
reports of immigrants who have committed crimes.

The propaganda has nothing to do with reality. Crimes
are committed by both Swedes and immigrants. The victims of crime are both Swedes and immigrants. And the
violent treatment of women is not culture-specific—even
if the National Democrats and certain journalists writing
on the leader pages of *Dagens Nyheter* have joined forces in
claiming that there is something special about the violent
treatment of women by immigrant men.

In this respect the propaganda goes against all scientific research in that area. The reality can be summed up
in the conclusion that eight out of ten women exposed
to violence are married to or living with a man born in
Sweden. (The statistic comes from "*Slagen dam—mäns*

våld mot kvinnor i jämställda Sverige" [Battered Women—Men's Violent Treatment of Women in Equality-Sweden], Eva Lundgren et al., Uppsala University, 2001.)

It is worth repeating: the violent treatment of women is not a culture-specific phenomenon, but rather the effect of men's need to control women. A perpetrator of such violence is probably just as likely to hold left-wing as right-wing political opinions. It might be true to add that the more sectarian and socially isolated a group is, the greater the risk factor for individual activists turning to violence—a pattern we recognize from Knutby,[1] Jim Jones's suicide sect in Guyana[2] and dozens of similar groups all over the world. And the National Democrats are very much a sect.

The hypocrisy factor within the "nationalist" movement is very high. As the movement is racist, all its activities are based in one way or another on conducting propaganda against immigrants, Jews, homosexuals and any other groups regarded as a threat to "Swedish culture."

There is also an attempt to build up an image of "Swedes" as morally superior. But, of course, the difference between theory and practice is dramatic. At *Expo* we would have no time to spare for anything else if we were forced to report on every occasion that a Nazi beats up his partner, or travels over to Tallinn to practice multicultural intercourse with teenage prostitutes provided by local Nazi pimps.

Expo journalist Mikael Ekman stumbled on one of the most fascinating examples of double standards when he undertook an investigation into the Swedish pornography industry for the TV3 program "Insider." He toured Stockholm with a hidden camera and visited several porn shops.

Imagine his surprise as he was investigating a shelf of pornographic films to suddenly find himself face to face with one of the key people in the anti-Jewish Nazi organization Info-14.

Info-14 and the National Democrats cooperate on practical matters such as the arrangements for the Salem March every year, and both the groups specialize in targeting immigrants who commit crimes. They take particular pleasure in exposing sexually related crime, and claim to be combating pedophiles and homosexuals, even implying that there is a link between those categories.

Friends of law and order will doubtless be wondering what the high-ranking moral activist from Info-14 was doing in the porn shop. Well, he worked there. The scenario was made no better by the fact that the shop is owned by a homosexual Jew, and that it specializes in gay pornography.

Tor Paulsson has made a virtue out of presenting himself and his family in National Democratic propaganda as a confidence-inspiring model of the happy Swedish family—in contrast with all the culturally unreliable dark-skinned men who rape, beat up women and commit honor killings on their children. Together with his partner he used to play that role on election posters even when he was still a member of the Sweden Democrats.

As if that were not enough, Tor Paulsson is in practice the party leader, even if Anders Steen formally attaches his name to that post.

The National Democrats have based all their activities on Tor Paulsson's activist strategy, in which the fight against the violent treatment of women (by immigrants) is a cornerstone.

In pamphlet after pamphlet the National Democrats portray themselves as the party that cares for families, the country and our culture—and which does battle with established politicians who threaten that ideal image.

The National Democrats have realized the desperate nature of their situation. At a stroke, Tor Paulsson's punches have thrust the party into a crisis in which the whole country questions their credibility. The N.D. have reacted quickly and already announced on their website that Paulsson must quit the party. An even better move would be to shut down the party altogether.

In normal circumstances the National Democrats can find mitigating circumstances or conspiracies that excuse the use of violence by activists, as when their youth leader Marc Abramsson was recently given a stiff sentence for his role in the attack on last year's Pride festival. But Tor Paulsson's punches are so palpable that it is difficult to find any mitigating circumstances. Even if the party ideologue Vavra Suk makes a lame attempt to give Tor Paulsson's violent treatment of a woman a cultural spin when he compares Swedish violence towards women with immigrants' violence towards women: "The difference is one's attitude to what is right and what is wrong. If Tor Paulsson has in fact done what he is accused of having done, I am convinced that he will regret it. People from the Muslim culture do not regret their actions," Vavra Suk told *Dagens Nyheter*.

The party leader Anders Steen, who happens to be Tor Paulsson's stepfather, described the assault as a "family tragedy." He is not usually so generous when commenting on similar cases of assault when the perpetrator is a culture-specific immigrant.

Notes

1. The Knutby Murders is one of the most notorious cases in Swedish criminal history. In January 2004, a 30-year-old man was found seriously injured after being shot in the head and chest. Two hours later his employee and neighbor was found shot dead. The murdered woman was married to Helge Fossmo, a pastor at a local Pentecostal church. The next day a 26-year-old woman who had worked as a nanny in the pastor's family confessed to both shootings. Two weeks later, the pastor was arrested, together with the wife of the wounded man. The police had discovered that they were lovers. Both were suspected of instigating the murder and the murder attempt, but the wife of the wounded man was never charged.

2. Jim Jones was the leader of the sect the Peoples Temple. On November 18, 1978, 909 of its members committed suicide in Jonestown, Guyana. The incident ranks among the largest mass suicides in history.

SWEDISH AND UN-SWEDISH
VIOLENCE TOWARDS WOMEN

From *Debatten om hedersmord*
(The Debate on Honor Killings)
Svartvitt Förlag, 2004

A young woman in Sweden is at the start of her life. She has many plans for the future to choose from: she is interested in horse-riding, in dogs and taking care of animals, and she is considering the possibility of training as a veterinary surgeon. She is also so physically attractive that she earns some welcome money as a photographic model for advertisements.

She is also dependent on a considerably older man with whom she has a close relationship. In order to be able to achieve her plans for the future—no matter what career she decides to go in for—the older man must give way and release his hold over her. She finds herself in the middle of a process of liberation in which it has taken her a long time to dare to take the step of making it clear that she will no longer allow him to control her life.

Her feelings of unease regarding the man's influence over her life have been growing for some time. The man has a powerful need to control situations, and wants to regulate her relations with her friends of her own age. She is also physically afraid of the man. He has a criminal background with links to a foreign and well-documented crime syndicate. He is most probably well aware that if the young woman is allowed to make her own decisions about her future, his position will be very much undermined. He has made it clear to her that if she rebels against him, she will find herself in deep trouble. He threatens to spoil her appearance by branding her, and he threatens to kill her.

In the autumn of 2001 the conflict between the young woman and the older man comes to a head. After much anguish and fear for her physical safety, the young woman makes up her mind to put her foot down. She rebels. She makes it clear that she no longer wants anything to do with him. She also tells her friends about his threatening behavior, which he interprets as a disgraceful betrayal that puts his honor in question.

At the end of 2001 the man pays a visit to the young woman, who at the time is living in a remote cottage on the outskirts of their town.

We cannot know exactly how that visit came about— whether the young woman gave way to his demands and threats and entreaties and voluntarily agreed to meet him, or whether he simply turned up unannounced. The answer is irrelevant anyway. What we do know, and what is relevant, is that during the course of the visit the young woman was attacked by the older man. The attack was planned, for he had taken with him the equipment he needed to achieve his ends. The woman was assaulted grievously for several hours. She was tortured with an electric pistol among other things, and subjected to repeated sexual assaults. In the end she was choked and killed. The post-mortem shows that she put up desperate resistance.

Having carried out the deed, the man (we can assume) feels that he has satisfactorily recovered his honor and respect; and so the next stage can take place. He must tidy up the scene of the crime and remove the young woman's remains. So he takes out his mobile telephone and rings a relative of about his own age, a "director" in the recording industry. He explains his precarious position, and his friend promises to stand by him.

They help each other to remove all visible signs of torture, and wrap the young woman's body in chicken wire and iron chains, purchased the day before. They really want to sink the body in deep water, but it is late November and that plan would present too many logistical difficulties so it is abandoned. Instead they drive out to the Björkvik jetty on the island of Ingarö and dump the body in three meters of water. The very next day the body is discovered by a family with children who happen to be going for a walk along the jetty.

Her name was Melissa. She was murdered at Margaretalunds-vägen in Åkersberga in November 2001.

She was twenty-two years of age. The murderer's name was Torbjörn, a Stockholmer with a criminal record and contacts in criminal Hell's Angels circles. He was thirty-seven years of age and had been Melissa's "boyfriend" for two years. He was sentenced by the district court to life imprisonment, but felt himself badly done by and lodged an appeal. Torbjörn's friend—who may or may not have participated in planning the murder—is called Martin, and was sentenced to two years in prison for desecrating a grave.

Two months later Fadime was murdered. She was shot by her father, who was visiting her in Uppsala. The murder of Fadime, like the murder of Melissa shortly beforehand, became a long-running saga in the mass media; but the focus of articles and agitated emotions was dramatically different in the two cases.

In the case of Melissa the murder is treated as a piece of classical criminal journalism. Looking back, several of the articles read like titillating entertainment. Melissa's beauty is stressed by illustrating the articles with photographs taken from her modeling portfolio. Several of the articles maintain that she used to wear black leather trousers and flirted with death-metal music and Satanism. The description of her stresses her sexuality, while her murderer is portrayed of course as an object of hatred—he weighs 140 kilos and has tattoos all over his body. Needless to say, the reader wonders how a young and so unusually pretty girl could possibly have been the partner of such a man.

By contrast, the description of Fadime is severe, almost chaste. The murder is presented as an ideological or religious act, and does not follow the traditional pattern of crime journalism.

Nevertheless, there are obvious parallels between the murders of Melissa and Fadime.

In both cases a beautiful, outgoing young woman with a zest for life is dependent on an older man—Fadime on her father and Melissa on her boyfriend. Both cases involved older men with a need to control younger women who were in the process of breaking free. In both cases gender and sexuality play prominent albeit different roles. In both cases the women had been subjected for long periods to increasing unease linked with death threats. In both cases their rebellion was punished by death.

There are also differences between the cases. According to the mass media and concurring with the court judgment, the murder of Melissa was a cruel and premeditated killing linked with torture, but also an obviously "insane act" based on jealousy. The boyfriend simply could not tolerate Melissa going her own way and planning her own future outside his influence. But the murder of Fadime was a "culturally determined honor killing." Her father simply could not tolerate Fadime going her own way and mapping out her own future irrespective of his wishes.

"Melissa murders" are not unusual in Sweden. Statistics indicate between fifteen and twenty murders every year in which the main circumstances are approximately similar: threats, dependence, ill-treatment and violence. Every year Swedish women flee for their lives and seek protection wherever they can find it—in remote villages, with friends or in one of the refuges for women, of which there are more than two hundred, from Haparanda in the far north to Ystad in the far south. In other words, we live in a country where Swedish women need two hundred special refuges whose main task is to provide protection from violent men, mainly from within their own family. We also know that only a small percentage of violently treated women turn to a women's refuge for help.

Every year Swedish society produces a new generation of threatened women who can testify to the lack of legal rights and the lukewarm interest shown by the police and other authorities. Evidence of the lack of legal rights for Swedish women is interesting in this context. In the debate about honor killings it is claimed specifically that legislation in Muslim countries (as distinct from the culturally advanced legal situation in Sweden) favors and legitimizes violence on the part of men.

This systematic violence directed at women—for systematic violence is exactly what it is, and what it would be called if it affected to a similar extent trade unionists, or Jews, or the disabled—is never regarded as a "cultural problem" in Sweden. Indeed, one could ask if it is regarded as a problem at all, apart from in a strictly legal context. The violent treatment of women is illegal, and hence the perpetrator can reckon with some form of stiff reprisals after any such acts are committed.

But there is practically nothing available written by a Swedish social polemicist in which the writer tries to explain the murder of Melissa from a Swedish cultural-anthropological or broader cultural perspective. Such argumentation is reserved exclusively for "immigrants," "Kurds" or "Muslims," who can be studied in relation to Swedish culture.

It is of course impossible to compare the violent treatment of women and suggest that one murder is more cruel than another. In that respect Fadime and Melissa were sisters. An objection frequently made by supporters of a "cultural-anthropological" approach—and the argument is legitimate to a certain extent—is that a fundamental difference between the murders of Melissa and Fadime is that few Swedish murders are encouraged by relations, close family and close friends. This, it is argued, is the difference that makes the murder of Fadime a culturally influenced "honor killing" and the murder of Melissa a run-of-the-mill Swedish affair.

But this thesis is not completely true either. Surprisingly often—as was the case in the Melissa murder—violence is encouraged by individuals in the killer's close circle of friends. It is difficult to find any other explanation for the willingness of friends of Swedish women-murderers to assist in tidying up the scene of the crime and in disposing of the body.

There are plenty of examples of this. A case that attracted a lot of attention a few years ago was the woman who committed suicide at the home of a notorious middle-aged swindler, known as the Count. When the Count's girlfriend died on his sofa after repeated quarrels, he did not telephone the police or ring for an ambulance, but instead contacted three male friends, who quickly appeared on the scene with hacksaws to butcher her body. Then, in accordance with good old Swedish traditions, the men drove around on country roads north of Stockholm and in Roslagen, dumping her remains bit by bit.

This case has not been subjected to cultural-anthropological scrutiny either.

Nor has Catrine da Costa been mentioned by any of those who argue in favor of a "cultural-anthropological" explanation. Why not? Might it have something to do with the fact that Catrine was a prostitute, and hence a "legitimate" victim of male violence? It should be stressed once again that it is not the case that the murderers risk no legal reprisals. If the pathologist well known throughout Sweden and the general practitioner had committed murder (a part of the male network contest this) and been found guilty of murder, they would doubtless have been sentenced to life imprisonment.

But the point is that in this case it is not a question of a "lone madman" but possibly of "two lone madmen" who, according to the district court, found it socially and culturally acceptable to butcher a violated female body.

Even if violence or the threat of violence against a Swedish woman is not seen as politically correct, those in circles closest to what is going on—both men and women—are often known to close their eyes to it.

When the cries from the next-door flat become too disturbing, those in favor of law and order turn up the volume of their television sets. In such cases, men's violence towards women must be regarded as something that is annoying, to be sure, but nevertheless a socially acceptable pattern of behavior—*we can't interfere in what is happening in people's private lives, and if she doesn't enjoy being beaten up then she can always move out.* And how often do we hear in court the explanation that in fact she is the one who provoked the violence, and that she has only herself to blame? *You have to feel sorry for Bertil, who's had to put up with a witch like that for so many years before things came to a head.*

To a certain extent that way of thinking also applied to Melissa's murder. When it became known that she had flirted with death-metal music and Satanism in her choice of clothes and lifestyle, journalists quietly discovered a "rational" explanation for her death. She had chosen her boyfriend/murderer of her own freewill. Was she looking for a titillating experience? Was she even complicit in her own killing?

Another difference between the murder of Melissa and the murder of Fadime is that while the former has already been forgotten, Fadime has attracted international attention.

It is an excellent thing that Fadime should be noticed in this way. But for God's sake, Melissa should not be forgotten. Nor should Gerd, Solveig, Helén, Elisabeth, Anita, Jenny, Kristina, Marianne, and the hundreds of other girls who have been victims and continue to be victims of male violence that has nothing to do with cultural norms. Here in Sweden. Every day, year after year. Without it occurring to a single cultural anthropologist that this is a conditioned reflex in Swedish men. And without a single Swedish political party in the 2002 election debate grasping the idea that this is a national social problem that must be addressed as the highest of priorities. Despite all the attention paid to them in the media, neither Fadime nor Melissa featured in the Swedish election debates—with the possible exception of the Social Democratic Youth Organization, of which Fadime had been a member.

Nevertheless, Fadime's shadow hovered over the election. What persisted following the debate about honor killings was a demand for language tests and the stricter treatment of immigrants who were culturally un-Swedish.

The murder of Fadime gave rise to an intense debate in the media about which a lot could be said. Media coverage took place within the framework of the Swedish "cultural model," with all that implies about racist and ethnocentric prejudices.

The media have the ability—and this is their strength—to focus on a currently relevant topic and retain the attention of a whole nation for a certain length of time. The targets of this sort of focused journalism often (and dismissively) refer to it as "media drive." This kind of objection is sometimes justified—how interesting is it really that a politician is caught buying a bar of chocolate with money provided by the taxpayer?

However, it *is* interesting to note that nearly all the big media drives for the last ten years have been aimed at female politicians: the Anna-Greta Leijon affair,[1] Gudrun Schyman's alcohol habits,[2] the Laila Freivalds apartment business,[3] Mona Sahlin's credit card,[4] Yvonne Ruwaida's taxi rides,[5] and so on. The only exception in recent years is probably Jan O. Karlsson's[6] shot at the media that hit the post—but then, he was the Immigration Minister and hence an obvious target for all and sundry.

The difference in the way the media treat men and women is striking. Yvonne Ruwaida was forced to run the gauntlet for not producing receipts for her taxi rides, while Sten Andersson, then a member of the Moderate Party, was merely mentioned in a single notice four centimeters long for exactly the same offence. Not even the fact that around the same time Andersson defected from the conservatives to the Sweden Democrats roused journalists from their slumbers. Can anyone imagine the belligerent headlines if Yvonne Ruwaida had announced that she was defecting to a racist party?

But media drives can also have a positive effect, focusing on questions that would otherwise slip by unnoticed outside small groups of activists with limited resources and associations with a special interest. The murder of Fadime was such a case.

It meant that the situation in which a large number of immigrant women find themselves was for the first time widely noticed, and taken seriously outside their own circles. It meant that Kurdish men's attitudes towards women were scrutinized. It meant that the lack of justice meted out to women was demonstrated in a comprehensible way. It meant that attention was drawn to the inability of the police to provide protection, and the nonchalance of the authorities; it gave rise to major demonstrations and forced even the government to take action.

It is also obvious that the media, whatever their political views, published their articles from a male point of view, and that much of the reporting came close to the borderline of what is acceptable when the attitude towards women of Muslims and Kurds was treated in a generalized way.

In this book I have deliberately used the expressions the death of *Fadime* and the death of *Melissa*. This is how the Swedish mass media reported them—which in itself ought to warrant a cultural-anthropological reaction.

Fadime's surname was never used by the mass media. She was presented to the whole of the Swedish nation simply as *Fadime*. Emerging from nowhere, she was transformed into a subject of national concern, and was buried without anybody even remembering her surname.

Try it yourself. Ask anyone in the street. Everybody knows exactly who Fadime was, but few people outside the circle of Kurds, gender researchers, journalists and officials employed by authorities responsible for immigration will be able to tell you her full name.

This situation was established during the days following the murder by newspaper after newspaper. *Expressen* devoted its placards, front page, leading articles and eight pages of text written by seven different reporters to "The murder of Fadime." Her photograph was published, and detail after detail of the murder was discussed without a single reporter ever mentioning her surname.

Aftonbladet carried thirteen pages written by fourteen journalists, male and female. None of them indicated that she had a surname. One of these writers was Kurdo Baksi, who is my friend and hence a part of my male network, as well as being the publisher of this book. Even he was carried along by the idiom used in the media drive. On the other hand, he was the first person to notice and comment on the fact that Fadime had no surname.

And so it went on in newspaper after newspaper—*Dagens Nyheter, Göteborgs-Posten, Sydsvenskan* and others. It was not until Friday, January 25—four days after the murder—that we discovered Fadime actually did have a surname. Her full name was mentioned in passing in a figure caption in *Expressen*, almost by accident. That was the day Fadime's murderer was exposed. Her father—the man. He had a surname, and so readers were able to conclude that the victim also had one.

The remarkable thing is that even now that Fadime has acquired a surname, a pattern has been established in the media. In all the articles about her life, thoughts, feelings and person she has remained Fadime. It is only in a few articles that deal specifically with the murderer and the legal process that Fadime is given a surname.

Her name was *Sahindal*. Fadime Sahindal.

Her sister in death was called *Nordell*. Melissa Nordell.

A person's name is important. It is a part of his or her identity. The reaction of all those who discussed the death of Fadime Sahindal is understandable. No one was untouched by it. She could have been a sister or a friend of anybody at all, and in her death she became familiar to the whole of the Swedish nation. But only and always to call her simply Fadime shows a lack of respect. It suggests that she was a child or a domestic pet, defenseless and naive. Dogs have only one name. People have two names. The combination of first name and surname creates a person's identity.

In this context the sex roles are almost over-explicit in crime journalism. When the victim is a man, both his first name and surname are always used. We know about the murder of Björn Söderberg in Sätra, of Gerard Gbeyo in Klippan, of Peter Karlsson in Västerås and so on. No editor would ever dream of writing a placard with the text "The Murder of Björn" when the man referred to is Björn Söderberg. But when the victim is a woman it is normal to use only her first name. We have *Helén* in Höör, *Nathalie* in Sundsvall, *Melissa* in Åkersberga, and lots of others. Anyone trying to find out Melissa's surname by searching through *Aftonbladet's* web edition, for instance—where there are several articles about the murder—will spend a long time looking.

How the name is used also defines status and social position. Olof Palme was well known to all Swedish people— but there has never been a single placard trumpeting out a message concerning "The Murder of Olof." On the few occasions that only the first name is used, it has always been in comments made by a very close personal friend of Olof Palme's—former Foreign Secretary Sten Andersson, for instance. And this is also part of a pattern. If Fadime had been a man, no journalist—male or female—would have referred to her using only the first name.

But Fadime Sahindal had an identity over and above that of a child or a dog. She was an adult. She was studying to become a sociologist. She was a Social Democrat. She was twenty-six years old and single. She had her roots in Kurdistan but had grown up in Sweden.

And she was a woman. That is why she was murdered. The murder of Fadime Sahindal gave rise to one of the most furious debates seen in Sweden for many years. At times it seemed to be irreconcilable.

As the debate ceased to occupy most people's consciousness and was relegated to a few specialist journals— the Sahindal murder will only be discussed again in the media in connection with its anniversary and on occasions when some other Kurdish girl is attacked in similar circumstances—the matter is now closed and filed away in the social climate that applied before the murder. This means that nothing of real value was achieved, that none of the pledges made at the time will be developed or become part of a new political order.

That is why Fadime Sahindal became a non-person in the election campaign when all parties had an excellent opportunity to discuss what measures they would introduce to improve the situation of vulnerable women. Instead we had a debate about immigrants being required to pass tests in the Swedish language before they could apply for citizenship.

Cynical? Yes, of course. The question that comes to mind two years later is this: what was the debate actually about?

Its starting point can probably be described as pent-up fury. Women are fed up of being ill-treated, threatened, raped and murdered. It was time to cleanse the Augean stables. Since Fadime Sahindal was of Kurdish origin it was only natural that attention should focus on male Kurdish networks and attitudes. A number of Kurdish gentlemen acknowledged a degree of guilt, while others protested their innocence. Several Kurds who neither sympathize with nor defend honor killings were subjected to vicious attacks. The magazine and publishing house *Svartvitt* (Black and White), for instance, received abusive telephone calls and murder threats. The debate and the media coverage were characterized by generalizations and racist conceptions.

The murder of Fadime Sahindal drew attention to the concept of honor killing—which supports the notion that a man's honor is located between a woman's legs. Various polemicists in this book have defined and explained the concept in more comprehensible terms, but the above will suffice as a starting point for this contribution.

However, the debate took a course that did not follow the usual pattern. Instead of focusing on men's need to control situations, the violent treatment of women and the absence of justice for women, it concentrated on whether or not the murder of Fadime Sahindal took place for cultural reasons—if there was something in specific Kurdish cultural patterns that makes Kurdish men want to murder their daughters.

The arguments were divided into two fairly distinct categories. One held to a "traditional" explanation (simplified here), that Fadime Sahindal was murdered for sexist reasons—that it made no practical difference that the murderer was a Kurd, a Muslim and also her father, just as it was irrelevant that Melissa Nordell's murderer was an overweight Swedish boor with tattoos.

Supporters of this way of thinking (with certain variations) maintained that the masculine urge to control women (not just to control women's sexuality but to take away their very right to exercise control over their body and their life) was the reason for the murder, and that this is a global and not a culturally specific problem. This explanation fits the murders of both Melissa Nordell and Fadime Sahindal. The cause lies in male-dominated society—"patriarchal structures"—where laws are structured to favor men and place women in an unjustly vulnerable position. The solution is to safeguard and strengthen democracy.

The other line of argument, which will be labeled here the "cultural-anthropological" approach, argued that the murder of Fadime was specifically related to her murderer being a Kurd and a Muslim. There is a significant divergence of opinion among followers of this line, with polemicists putting forward arguments that are almost irreconcilable with others.

Between these positions there was also a variety of views, including several put forward by Kurdish women. This article, how- ever, will be concerned with only the "cultural-anthropological" argument, the basis of a large number of contributions to the debate.

One of the main contributions appeared in *Dagens Nyheter*, written by the cultural anthropologist Mikael Kurkiala, who is a researcher at the University of Uppsala, well known for his study of the Navajo Indians in North America. Kurkiala maintained in sweeping terms that reactions aroused by "the persecution of young, often Kurdish, women—such as the murder of Fadime Sahindal—are opportunistic and self-opinionated. Above all they avoid the arguments put forward by the persecuted women themselves, whose testimony is all too uncomfortable."

Kurkiala's article was entitled *"Den stora skräcken för skillnader"* (The Great Fear of Differences). He argued that since multiculturalism and multiplicity are politically correct key-words in Sweden, it is remarkable that so many of the debaters expressed antagonism towards and an "almost panic-stricken fear" of differences. In other words, those who argued that the male-dominated society was at the root of the murder of Fadime were scared of uncovering any cultural differences between Swedes and Kurds.

Kurkiala's standpoint is not new or unknown: in many contexts and in various forms it has been argued by the Front

National in France, by the Danskt Folkeparti (Danish People's
Party) in Denmark and by the Sweden Democrats in Sweden.
For the record I should make it clear that I am not suggesting that Kurkiala is a fascist or sympathizes with any of the
above-mentioned political organizations: these parties are
named here merely because they are part of the only political
movement that has consistently, over many years, made an
ideology out of precisely this ethnocentric cultural relativism.

To simplify somewhat, it could be said that right-wing
extremists support the thesis that blood (i.e. an individual's
makeup) and his or her cultural and ethnic origin constitute
a person's value. This is an extreme point of view based on
racist conceptions and national stereotypes. In the normal
world populated by democratic people, we generally believe
that education, social competence and capacity for empathy
make for a person's value—and not skin color, language or
choice of clothing. That is the difference.

The Sweden Democrats (S.D.) were founded in 1979
under the designation Bevara Sverige Svenskt (B.S.S.—
Keep Sweden Swedish), and soon became known as a hard-
line racist campaign organization. The party took the name
Sweden Democrats in 1988, and today they are the most
successful "nationalist party" since the 1930s.

For most of the party's existence—from 1979 until the
election campaign of 1998—their dominant influence has
come from Nazi groups. During the 1990s, however, the
party has toned down the more obscene aspects of its program to make itself a more viable alternative for Swedish
voters. The wearing of uniforms at public meetings has
been banned, and the party manifesto has been reworded

in order to appeal more to the protest voters on whom the party hopes to build its political future. This strategy by the S.D. echoes the pattern established by corresponding parties abroad. The far right has realized that excessively militant and crude rhetoric scares voters away, and creates legal problems when members are charged with agitation against a minority, unlawful threat or instigation of rebellion. Instead, they have concentrated on stirring up racist attitudes that already exist in Swedish society.

The key to "the new racism" was the decision by nationalist groups in the 1970s to abandon the racial biology that the movement had embraced enthusiastically for over fifty years. The old fascist leader Per Engdahl expressed it most clearly in his journal *Vägen Framåt* (The Way Forward) when he stated in 1979 that science and genetics had proved that there were no differences between races. He admitted that, in view of this, the movement had been wrong throughout its existence—but claimed in the next breath that this did not mean that racists needed to abandon racism: they should now, rather, stress the cultural differences between "them" and "us."

By far the most important questions in the nationalist movement's thinking today are:

Islamophobia

The creation of myths about Muslims'—and in particular Arabs'—behaviour patterns, beliefs, lifestyle and cultural reliability has replaced using Jews as the major target for hate propaganda. Anti-Semitism has been toned down and is restricted mainly to being the hallmark of openly Nazi organizations such as the National Socialist Front, Blood &

Honour and Nationalist Youth. Anti-Semitism does persist among the more "respectable" organizations, not least the National Democrats (N.D.), but it has been rephrased in terms of conspiracy theories involving "Freemasons," "luminaries," "cosmopolitans," or similar groups. It is claimed that the main threat now comes from Arabs and Muslims.

The threat to culture

All extreme-right groups, both Nazis and National Democrats, preach that immigration is a threat to Swedish culture. Precisely what is meant by "Swedish culture" is never defined—that would create endless logistical problems—but there is an underlying presumption that "our culture" is better than "their culture."

Criminality

The most effective propaganda describes immigrants as gangs of criminals. Hence the Sweden Democrats and National Democrats fill their home pages with descriptions of how immigrants rob, smuggle, steal and commit acts of violence. The key ingredient in this propaganda concerns rape and the violent treatment of women. The Sweden Democrats shamelessly suggest that immigrants do not have the same "enlightened attitude towards women" as Swedes, and that immigration now presents a threat to Swedish women, since immigrants cannot control their sexuality and are disposed to commit rape and particularly gang rape. And so the Sweden Democrats have evolved their most effective slogan: *Stop gang rape—stop immigration*. At the same time they describe themselves as the only party that "protects women's rights" and Swedish "respect for women."

Democracy

The real villains of the piece, however, are not immigrants, but "the anti-Swedish elite" pulling the strings of power: it is they who have betrayed the Swedish people and sold out the country to a foreign occupying power—immigrants. The power elite comprises corrupt politicians from all parties, those in authority, journalists, feminists, homosexuals, Marxists, "left-wing radical opinion-formers" and others who have transformed Sweden from a democracy into a dictatorship.

All the established parties belong to "the traitors" who, to quote from a Sweden Democrat propaganda leaflet, are ruining our country and "sacrificing the Swedish people on the altar of multiculturalism."

The Sweden Democrats also maintain that immigration costs the country fantastic amounts—the latest claim is 260 million kronor per year. This led to a debate recently in the Eslöv local council which resulted in the Conservative Mikael Kourtzman losing his patience and exclaiming: "What a lot of disgusting rubbish!"

One extract from Mikael Kurkiala's article could have been copied word-for-word from any Sweden Democrat propaganda text:

In many respects our society has been dismantled socially and morally. Class differences are increasing, the politically untouchable holy trinity of "education, welfare and health care" is hovering on the verge of total collapse at the same time as those in charge of our financial well-being are flourishing at the expense of the less well-off. Degrading and stereotypical images of masculinity and femininity overwhelm us every time we switch on our television sets and consumerism has become the cure-all with regard to our existential angst and permanent identity crisis. That is precisely why it is important that we maintain clear-sighted perspicacity and examine critically the basic values on which our society is built.

The Sweden Democrats must be cheering. That is precisely what they preach in their propaganda. Society and security in the form of health care, education and welfare are being dismantled, while the corrupt powers that be flourish at the expense of the Swedish people. Consumerism has become an anesthetic that prevents us from getting to grips with our identity crisis—the fact that Swedish culture is being destroyed.

The Sweden Democrats, like the Front National in France, know that traditional race-biological arguments are a no-go area for politicians, so instead the strategy concentrates on encouraging opposition to immigration from outside Europe by stirring up suspicions about immigrant culture. In this respect, the form—not the content—of the Fadime debate was worth its weight in gold for a budding racist party that apparently had so many of its hobby-horses backed by the mainstream mass media and respectable polemicists. *There you are, you see—that's exactly what we have always said. Now even cultural anthropologists are saying the same thing. Mass immigration leads to contempt for women.* And so the party launches their slogan: *Stop gang rape—stop immigration.*

Åsa Elden, a sociologist at Uppsala University whose 2003 doctoral thesis was entitled *"Heder på liv och död: Våldsamma berättelser om rykten, oskuld och heder"* (Honor in Life and Death: Violent Stories about Reputation, Innocence and Honor), is one of Sweden's most knowledgeable experts on the subject of honor killings. Her assertion that the concept has acquired misleading cultural resonance and is actually about violence towards women drew attacks from not only supporters of the cultural-anthropological explanation but also the Sweden Democrats. The S.D. home page commented:

> The forced attempt to turn a cultural question into a feminist one is pretty lame. In Swedish culture there is an awareness of equality which results in injustice between men and women being exposed and dealt with, even if the whole matter has been undermined by the equality feminism of the last decade. Where is this awareness or the will to develop it in Kurdish or similar cultures? Honour killings do not exist in Swedish culture. Nor are women declared incapable of managing their own affairs or inferior to men in Sweden. [...] Honour killings are an outcome of a multicultural society. The mutual enrichment alleged to be the result of cultures coming together had virtually no positive effect compared with the negative effects that now dominate the rule of law in Sweden.

When Per T. Olsson, editor-in-chief of *Sydsvenska Dagbladet*, wrote that "immigrants have, and should have, the

right to uphold their own culture and traditions [. . .] but
Swedish culture will accept no compromise when it comes
to customs and criminal acts," he received a response from
the Sweden Democrat Kenneth Sandberg from Kävlinge:
"Thus spake the representative of multicultural society.
[. . .] We should have no illusions about Per T. Olsson *et
consortes* placing on the agenda the only relevant and ade-
quate question, which is how is it possible that these groups
are accommodated in Sweden?"

Gabriella Johansson, leader of the S.D.'s women's organization Aurora (which seems to exist only on paper in an
otherwise extremely male-dominated party), managed to
turn Fadime's murder into party propaganda:

> I think Fadime was courageous. She expressed her disagree-
> ment when her family called their new homeland morally
> degenerate and her Swedish boyfriend unworthy. She became
> a model for all young immigrant women who choose to
> live as Swedes in Sweden, as should be the norm for people
> who come here and choose to stay. No multiculturalism, but
> assimilation. In current circumstances, i.e. mass immigration
> and low admission requirements, Fadime is an example for
> all immigrants.

Even Pia Kjaersgaard entered the debate. She claimed that:

> from the Kurdish father's barbaric view of life, the killing was
> honourable.
>
> Sweden's multicultural experiment, which we others
> have been watching for years with considerable doubts and

scepticism, now seems to have received its most serious blow so far. That is good, but it is a pity that a young woman should have to lose her life before it happens. She was the victim of the multiculturalists' Utopia.

Kjaersgaard's comment teems with cultural chauvinism. Kurdish culture is *barbaric*. But, says Kjaersgaard, Fadime was really killed by the multicultural society—the failed experiment of allowing blacks into Sweden. And yet again it was the political elite who pulled the strings.

Stupid? Yes, of course. But six months later Sweden went to the polls. The Sweden Democrats increased the number of their local government seats from eight to fifty, and with 1.4 percent of the total vote established themselves as the largest party outside parliament. Kenneth Sandberg received more than 10 percent of the vote in the Kävlinge local elections. There has not been any cultural-anthropological study charting the links between these attitudes and S.D.'s progress.

Supporters of a "cultural-anthropological" explanation came out with several typical statements. One of them was that the opponents' aim was to "marginalize the murder of Fadime" by comparing it with all other attacks on women. Among those arguing along these lines was Mikael Kurki-ala, who implicitly suggested that those who criticized the "cultural-anthropological" explanation were in favor of honor killings, if not openly then covertly; or at least had a suspect attitude. And so the debate descended to a level where those accused were forced first to distance themselves from honor killings—which they had anyway been doing for years.

A recurrent tactic was to describe opponents as "male intellectuals." This was also advanced by Mikael Kurkiala, and has more to do with rhetoric than with factual argument. If the circumstances of being "male" and "intellectual" disqualify people from participating in the debate, then Kurkiala has excluded himself. But forgive me: Kurkiala actually wrote "*Kurdish male intellectuals*"—he himself, of course, is an emancipated Scandinavian, and so is allowed to take part for a while longer. Is the level of the debate sufficiently low?

A third repeated argument was that those who supported traditional feminism "were disregarding the opinions expressed by the girls affected." In sweeping terms reference was made to a chorus of angry Kurdish young women who had dared at last to speak out and criticize Kurdish culture.

Certainly, Kurdish culture can be criticized on many grounds, but that was not the point. For every Kurdish girl who asserted that honor killings were a part of Kurdish culture there were other Kurdish girls who asserted the opposite—that honor killings are an expression of the lack of democracy in a patriarchal society. Why were these voices not heard on television chat shows?

Fadime Sahindal herself never suggested that Kurdish culture was the specific cause of honor killings and the suppression of women. She indicated lack of democracy as the reason for the suppression of women. Lise Bergh, the government minister with responsibility for matters of integration and equality, described her meetings with Fadime Sahindal.

"Fadime was not only courageous, she was also very clever," said Bergh. "Fadime referred to several other problems in addition to culture and tradition. The importance of integration, the lack of knowledge about these questions on the part of Swedish authorities, the lack of protection in acute situations and shortcomings in the cooperation between various authorities were areas Fadime frequently talked about."

With hindsight, a fourth type of reasoning was one of the most perplexing aspects of the debate. Opponents of the "cultural-anthropological" explanatory model were accused of representing a "Marxist" or "left-wing radical" line. This was the starting point of Kurkiala's polemic: "Left-wing debaters and most of the Kurdish [male] intellectuals repeat as a mantra that the murder has nothing to do with culture, and dismiss all cultural explanations as nonsense or pure racism."

One would expect Sweden Democrats to make such an assertion. They call everything outside their ethnocentric sect existence "Marxism," encompassing everything from the Christian Democrat Youth Association to masked anarchists with paving slabs in their hands. Even more perplexing is that several of the normally intelligent and reasonable debaters, such as the cultural journalists on *Expressen*, repeat the same nonsensical argument, just as if they had been attending the S.D.'s training school.

To maintain that Fadime Sahindal was murdered because she was a woman in a patriarchal society and that this is a global (as distinct from culture-specific) problem has suddenly become a *left-wing Marxist line*. Astonishing. This is the conclusion that gender researchers have been putting forward for several decades. It is possible, of course, that the next stage is for gender research as a whole to be accused of being "Marxist" in order to be discounted. Why not? It is a thesis already espoused by the Sweden Democrats.

But the basic question remains: why should "Marxism" be raised as something to complain about? The inevitable conclusion is that "Marxists" defend honor killings. What is the specifically "Marxist" aspect of maintaining that violence carried out by men against women is a masculine and patriarchal phenomenon?

If this reasoning were to be taken to its logical conclusion, there would be a difference between "Marxists" (who argue that the violent treatment of women is caused by men's need to be in control) and "anti-Marxists" (should we be consistent and call them fascists?) who argue . . . what? This is never explained in the course of the debate.

Mikael Kurkiala is no doubt much cleverer than I am and his conclusion no doubt has a solid basis, but I have great difficulty in finding any party line in the Fadime debate. In fact the debaters labeled as some sort of "left-wingers" were split more or less down the middle with regard to the explanatory model they supported.

Among those accused of being "left-wing debaters" were Jan Guillou, Liza Marklund and Kurdo Baksi. If they are the "left wing," then to be consistent the opposite camp, including Sara Mohammad, Dilsa Demirbag-Sten, Nalin Pekgul and others, should be called "right-wing debaters." I doubt that they would feel flattered by that label. This is, of course, not a question of being left-wing or right-wing in a political debate. No doubt there are as many "liberals" as "Marxists" who reject the culture-relativistic reasoning, and similar numbers in each camp who accept it. Just as it is possible to find similar proportions of "socialists" and "non-socialists" who ill-treat women, and just as the violent treatment of women occurs among Swedes as well as Kurds.

The core of the "cultural-anthropological" explanatory model was set out in Mikael Kurkiala's article *"Den stora skräcken för skillnader"* (The Great Fear of Differences), where he stated that so many of the debaters expressed denial—a "panic-stricken fear" of being different. Kurkiala considered this remarkable because "multiculturalism" is "a politically correct keyword" in Sweden. That is where the debate went off the rails. Kurkiala ascribed to debaters views they did not hold but which came to dominate the subsequent rhetoric.

It is not that any of the debaters denied the existence of cultural characteristics.

Every Swede, Muslim or Kurd who took part in the debate knows that there are cultural differences—after all, a large part of discussions in recent decades concerned this. A constant topic for debate has been how integration can take place while respect for cultural characteristics is retained.

Kurkiala can thus rest secure in the knowledge that everybody recognizes that cultural differences exist. One need only to compare a Stockholmer with someone from the north of Sweden to be aware of variations in customs, ways of thinking and attitudes; and obviously there is greater divergence between Swedish culture and that of a Kurdish immigrant.

What the "traditionalists" maintained, however, was that violence towards women is not a cultural-specific characteristic, but part of a global masculine way of thinking. Opponents looked for the common denominator between

Melissa Nordell and Fadime Sahindal. They advocated a conclusion accepted by gender research—that women are murdered because patriarchal values are dominant throughout the world.

Violence towards women and sexist (and racist) attitudes have existed down the ages, in all countries and in all cultures. It was one of the reasons (along with clannish economic measures) that Birger Jarl introduced *kvinnofrid-slagor* (women's safety laws) in Sweden in the thirteenth century, and is why some eight hundred years later two hundred women's refuges are necessary in Sweden.

Of course the advocates of a "cultural-anthropological" line are right in saying that culture played a role in the murder of Fadime, in the sense that one can argue that in one form or another it is possible to define every human action as "cultural anthropology" (or "sociology" or "psychology," and so on). But that explanation is so sweeping it explains nothing at all. It is about as intelligent as stating that the Thirty Years War was fought for psychological reasons. Yes, indeed, but . . .

The "cultural-anthropological" explanation addresses only the form of the suppression, not the cause of it. The form may vary dramatically from Sicilian honor killing to Indian woman-burning to Swedish domestic violence on a Saturday night. But culture does not explain the underlying reasons why women worldwide are murdered, maimed, and forced into various forms of ritual behavior dictated by men—why men in patriarchal societies oppress women. In principle, the same violence is directed at male homosexuals, who in similar fashion are regarded as threatening male identity and superiority.

None of the supporters of the cultural-anthropological line has produced a single concrete suggestion for combating the violent treatment of women that differs in any way from proposals by other debaters. Both sides demand respect for the viewpoint of women immigrants that cries for help must be taken seriously, that the government must do something, that Mona Sahlin (or some other minister) must do her duty, that legal protection for women should be strengthened, and so on. But all these demands have been made over the years before the murder of Fadime Sahindal took place.

The reason for the absence of specific concrete proposals is simple. To use a "culture-anthropological" explanatory model in this connection is tantamount to stating that there is something wrong with, specifically, Kurdish culture and Kurdish men (and implicitly also with Kurdish women, even if this discussion was less noticeable two years ago).

If the problem is Kurdish "culture," then in the name of logic Kurdish culture should be opposed. This is exactly what is pro-posed by the Sweden Democrats and National Democrats, and by fascist ideologues such as Alain de Benoist, Jörgen Rieger, Roger Pearson and other racist biologists from classic racist cultural-anthropological journals such as *Mankind Quarterly*, *Neue Antropologi* and *Nouvelle École*. The basis of their reasoning is that "a war of the cultures" is taking place, and this dictates our human behavior.

When racists claim that there is a difference between "us" and "them," they mean that the common European cultural background is superior to that of other peoples. The violent treatment of Muslim women happens because dark-skinned Arabs are a culturally inferior race. (Let us ignore the fact that

Kurds are in fact an Indo-European people and not Arabs, as several Swedish debaters thought two years ago.)

Precisely how Kurdish culture should be opposed is, understandably, something none of the debaters chose to comment on (apart from the Sweden Democrats and National Democrats, of course). That was probably a sensible choice since to do otherwise could easily have led to a morass of racist conceptions and standpoints.

On the periphery of the debate, special forces are patrolling, ready to introduce ethnic cleansing. We saw examples of the consequences of the same kind of thinking during a large part of the 1990s when paramilitary far-right gangs in Bosnia devoted themselves to precisely this. The gangs were linked to parties such as the Serb Union Party, which was founded by the mafia boss Arkan, and the Serb Radical Party, the official sister party of the Sweden Democrats in the former Yugoslavia.

In the "cultural-anthropological" world there is no need to take into account the fact that hundreds of Swedish women every year retreat into women's refuges, while others find themselves attending A&E, or fleeing for their lives pursued by blond and blue-eyed men, lovers, relatives, brothers and fathers. On the contrary—Mikael Kurkiala denies that there is a connection. That is the point of his reasoning.

In this connection the "cultural-anthropological" explanatory model is convenient for Swedish society. It gives a free pass to Swedish men. All they need say is: "We are not Kurds." *Look, I'm an emancipated, modern, enlightened European who doesn't murder my daughter for the sake of honor, nor beat my wife.*

The suppression of women becomes synonymous with cultural impulses brought into the country by immigrants and hence the slogans are logical: *Stop violence—stop immigration. Save Swedish culture. Save Sweden.*

Those who suppress women do so for "cultural reasons"— not as a consequence of a masculine way of looking at the world.

Which brings us back to the sisterly relationship between Melissa Nordell and Fadime Sahindal and the dramaturgic problems that arose during the debate. Kurdish men assault women for "cultural" reasons. Swedish men assault women— for what reasons? None of the "cultural-anthropological" debaters have so far given a credible answer.

But the problem is not cultural. The problem is that women are murdered by men in male-dominated societies.

During the honor-killings debate common sense went on holiday and all comprehensible reasoning was turned upside down. In the cultural-relativistic confusion feminists were accused of being racists, and anti-racists of underestimating the importance of the violent treatment of women.

Those who supported cultural-relativistic reasoning forgot their basic course in feminism and ended up in an untenable theoretical mess. I suspect that many of the main players will back out of their ideological cul-de-sac in embarrassment. The retreat has already begun and many of the most absurd demands for a tightening up of citizenship laws and different scales of punishment depending on ethnicity, and so on, have already been withdrawn.

So there is reason to suppose that feminism and anti-racism will continue to walk hand-in-hand, even in the future.

Notes

1. Anna-Greta Leijon is a former Swedish Social Democratic politician. She was Minister of Justice from 1987 to 1988, when she was forced to step down after it was revealed that she had approved the Social Democrat Ebbe Carlsson's private investigation into the assassination of Olof Palme.

2. In the mid-2000s, the leader of the Left Party Gudryn Schyman elected to go public with her alcoholism.

3. Laila Ligita Freivalds is a Swedish Social Democratic politician and a former Swedish Minister for Justice and Minister for Foreign Affairs. In 2000 she was forced to resign as Attorney General when it emerged that she had bought an apartment that she had been occupying as a tenant, thus circumventing a controversial housing law that she had herself been partially responsible for introducing.

4. The so-called Toblerone Affair exploded in October 1995. The then Social Democratic candidate for party leader, Mona Sahlin, had used her official credit card to purchase goods for herself, among them two bars of Toblerone.

5. In January 2001 it was revealed that Yvonne Ruwaida, Member of Parliament for the Green Party, had been using her official credit card for two years without submitting a receipt. She had, among other things, travelled by taxi on expenses to a total of cost 70,000 kronor.

6. Jan O. Karlsson is a Swedish politician, former President of the European Court of Auditors and former government minister, who has been involved in media storms on a number of occasions over the course of his career. In November 2002 it was revealed that, in addition to his salary as Minister for Migration, he had been receiving a pension from his previous employment in the E.U. In the full glare of the media, his negative attitude towards journalists was soon revealed, and in an interview in 1988 he openly referred to them as a "disgusting pack."

TERROR AIMED AT
HOMOSEXUALS

Expo no. 4/5—1997

In the last decade three men have been murdered in Gothenburg by neo-Nazis. One of the victims was a sixty-year-old man going for an evening stroll near a café frequented by homosexuals. The murder took place in 1995, but it is only this year that the perpetrators have been arrested and taken to court.

Two notorious neo-Nazis, Daniel aged twenty-six and Peder aged nineteen, devote their time to an occupation that has become especially common in Gothenburg Nazi circles. They systematically assault homosexuals—or, as they put it, "beat up pooftas."

In the evening of June 7, 1995, they caught sight of the sixty-year-old artist Per Skoglund. The location was Nya Allén, near Järntorget square. This meant that Per Skoglund had only a few more minutes to live. Exactly how the assault took place has not yet been established. Daniel and Peder blame each other, and their versions are different.

Daniel insists that Peder gave him a bottle of tear gas, which he tried to use on Skoglund, but the spray mechanism was broken and he himself was hit full in the face by the gas. He claims that he was blinded, and thus unable to take part in the assault. Peder insists that the tear gas spray worked perfectly, that Daniel attacked Skoglund with it and continued the assault with punches and kicks until Skoglund died. Peder also claims that he tried to stop Daniel but was shoved away, and that after the murder he has feared for his own life.

The post-mortem report tells a clear story. Per Skoglund was subjected to an exceptionally rough assault. Bones were broken, internal organs injured and one lung punctured as a result of repeated kicks. His face and head suffered injuries so grievous they could only have been caused by somebody jumping up and down on his skull with both feet.

An ironic but scarcely relevant detail is that, contrary to what Daniel and Peder thought, Per Skoglund was not gay.

Proof disappeared

At the trial the court chose to believe Peder's version of what happened. There are several reasons for this.

Daniel is a notorious neo-Nazi and man of violence with a pronounced hatred of homosexuals. It is not the first time he has appeared in court. In 1990 he was sentenced to six years in prison for assisting another neo-Nazi to murder a gay man. Shortly after he was released he once again assaulted someone he assumed was homosexual. For his second "gay murder" Daniel was sentenced to eight years in prison.

Peder is also a notorious neo-Nazi and among his close friends are two skinheads who took part in the beating to death of John Hron in Kungälv in 1995.[1] But Peder has a much superior social status and a fair knowledge of how legal processes function. His father is one of the most senior police officers in Gothenburg.

As there was no technical evidence the trial was based on circumstantial evidence and the credibility of the defense offered.

Peder was found not guilty of murder, but was fined for protecting Daniel after the deed. However, in the closing stages of the trial it was disclosed that there had been technical evidence. When the police raided the homes of the accused men they found and confiscated the bottle of tear gas used in the murder and which Daniel claimed was broken. At some point between the house search and the forensic investigation, the bottle of tear gas vanished from the police station. The only piece of evidence that could have swayed the court in Daniel's favor had disappeared without trace.

Systematic terror

At first sight the murder of Per Skoglund might seem a case of pointless violence perpetrated by young people: gangsters attacking lone walkers at night. But that is not the case.

Daniel and Peder belong to a tight circle of neo-Nazis fixated on violence, who for many years have devoted themselves to attacking and assaulting homosexuals.

Almost every homosexual who has visited gay clubs in Gothenburg since the 1980s can recount at least one occasion on which they have been subjected to violence or threats of violence by neo-Nazis. The harassment is systematic, and society has been unable to provide protection for homosexuals.

Reports of incidents would fill several files, but attacks are often not even reported to the police. Doing so would mean that the victim's name would become public property, which would be tantamount to inviting further harassment.

Moreover, gays in Gothenburg know full well that reporting an incident to the police seldom leads to a charge and that if an attacker is in fact charged and found guilty the outcome is often so lenient—with a suspended sentence or small fine—that it seems pointless.

No rights

"Many of us often feel that we simply don't have any rights," a gay Gothenburger told *Expo*.

Most of the abuse and threats come from "ordinary" young people; but it is the neo-Nazis who have made the harassment systematic.

"Just suppose for a moment that some other group in society had been subjected to similar harassment over a number of years. Say that neo-Nazis had made a habit of beating up journalists, or politicians, or police officers. Or that three lawyers had been murdered for ideological reasons. Then things would have been very different."

Note

1. On August 16, 1995, a fourteen-year-old boy, John Hron, was brutally murdered by four Nazis. He and his friend had gone on a camping trip to Ingeltorpsjön outside Kungalv, north of Gothenburg. All of a sudden four young Nazis appeared, and after a long and brutal assault Hron was thrown into a lake, where he drowned.

THE ASSAULT ON FACUNDO UNIA

www.expo.se
August 24, 2003

National Democratic propaganda becomes more and more remarkable. The party, which has local council members in Södertälje and Haninge and wants to present itself as the patriotic front preserving Swedish values in suit and tie, must now find a credible explanation for why thirty-nine members of the party and its youth section, together with several known Nazis, were arrested for a violent attack on Gay Pride at the beginning of August.

Let us remind ourselves of the situation: several thousand people took part in this year's Pride Parade, and an estimated 100,000 spectators lined the route of the procession. In the middle of the march, about a hundred Nazis and National Democrats gathered to form a counter-demonstration at Slottsbacken with the rallying call "Crush the gay lobby." At first they stayed a reasonable distance away, but they approached the parade on the bridge at Skeppsbron.

And then, not unexpectedly, bottles were thrown and people assaulted. A child in a pram was hit by splinters of glass.

This behavior by the National Democrats was described by witnesses both in and outside the demonstration, by the media, by the police and by the King's royal guard as a violent and unprovoked attack on Gay Pride.

Who started the verbal abuse is not clear—it never is on occasions like this—which leaves the door open for accusations and counter-accusations. What is perfectly clear, however, is that Pride's press assistant Facundo Unia took action. He tried to calm the mood, and urged participants in the parade to hurry past the spot.

What is also perfectly clear is that activists from the National Democrats' youth section (N.D.U.) attacked Pride. There is no other way of explaining the fact that the N.D.U. gang assembled up the hill at Slottsbacken and then as a group moved down towards the gay parade, where participants were assaulted in full view of cameras and witnesses.

The person who suffered most was Facundo Unia. He tried to flee but stumbled and was surrounded by ten or so Nazis, who bombarded him with kicks and punches and blows with sticks. Bruised and bleeding, he was taken by ambulance to the Söder hospital.

As this violent behavior took place in the vicinity of the Royal Palace, first the King's High Guard intervened, and then the police. Groups of National Democrats stampeded through the Old Town. Thirty-nine people were detained and spent the rest of the gay parade sitting in Slottsbacken guarded by the police. Among them was Marc Abramsson, leader of the youth association N.D.U.

Those detained were eventually packed into a Stockholm Transport bus that drove around and dropped off the National Democrats in the sticks—so far out in the suburbs that it would be quite some time before they could make their way back to the city center and create more mischief.

So far, so good. It was a traditional if not very heroic end to activities involving our most patriotic young people. But one 25-year-old N.D.U. activist was arrested at the demonstration. He was remanded in custody on suspicion of causing grievous bodily harm.

Now the National Democrat propagandists needed to do some serious thinking to explain how all those young activists came to be bussed out of the city center in humiliating circumstances. The first explanation appeared like clockwork on the N.D. home page.

"N.D.U.'s counter-demonstration against the Pride Parade is attacked by a cascade of bottles." (August 2)

So, according to N.D., the fact that Pride's press assistant was so badly beaten that he had to be rushed to hospital was a result of the Pride Parade attacking the N.D. Which means that Facundo Unia's beating up was self-inflicted.

This despite the fact that not a single eye witness has been found who saw Pride marchers throwing bottles at the gang of skinheads and Nazis in Slottsbacken. Most of the Pride marchers were probably unaware of the N.D. presence until the N.D. attack took place. Nor did any of the television cameras present film any of the Pride marchers breaking ranks or throwing bottles at the National Democrats.

But this the N.D. explained (August 2) with the allegation that "certain of the mass media loyal to the government" merely reported Pride's version, that it was the N.D.U. activists throwing bottles rather than the Pride marchers. "It is logical that [the media] should keep the bottle-throwing gay activists behind their backs," wrote the N.D.

This explanation was evidently a little too vague. The very next day (August 3) N.D's home page asserted that it was "gay activists and left-wing extremists" who joined forces to throw glass bottles at N.D.U. members.

A couple of days later (August 5) N.D's home page reported that it was in fact Network Against Racism and (surprise, surprise) A.F.A. (Anti-Fascist Action).

While this propaganda war was raging the 25-year-old N.D.U. activist was held under lock and key, suspected of inflicting grievous bodily harm. He had previously distinguished himself in May in Uppsala, where he was involved in a fight with anti-racists. This time, after a week or so in custody, he was released, which gave rise to a new stage in the N.D's invention of headlines. It is now that the N.D. version of history becomes eyebrow-raising. The following headline invites several question marks:

"Wrongly arrested N.D.U.-member released and acquitted from suspicion of grievous bodily harm" (August 12).

According to the N.D., then, the 25-year-old was "wrongly arrested" and "acquitted." But in fact it was not as straightforward as that. The prosecutor considered that the young man was still suspected of assault, even if the classification had been reduced from G.B.H. to assault and battery. The Swedish constitution specifies that suspects may not be held in custody indefinitely, so it is pretty obvious that the 25-year-old had to be released from custody. But that does not mean, as the N.D. implies, that he has been "acquitted."

The article continues to walk the tightrope between fact and fantasy. The anonymous N.D. propagandist writes: "In connection with the attack by the anarchistic organization A.F.A. in cooperation with gay activists on the National Democratic Youth (N.D.U.) counter-demonstration at the Gay Pride parade . . ." N.D.'s story has now changed significantly from its first version. It is now no longer Pride that "attacks," but A.F.A., cooperating with Pride. And so N.D. reaches new remarkable conclusions:

> The taking into custody [of the 25-year-old] was simply an attempt by the leaders of the Stockholm Police force to placate their political overlords in the establishment who were calling for vigorous measures to subdue those, i.e. the N.D.U., who had been impudent enough to assert their constitutional right to demonstrate against the establishment's Gay Pride ceremony. [. . .] The only reason why the 25-year-old was arrested is that two lesbians from the Gay Pride procession testified to police on the spot that the 25-year-old was behind the assault. (August 12)

This paragraph contains so many peculiarities of logic
that it ought to be used as a sample text in nationalist rhetoric at the Department of Argumentation Analysis at some
university or other.

The N.D. claims in all seriousness that the 25-year-old
was taken into custody because establishment politicians
put police chiefs under pressure. Any citizen with the slightest inkling of how legal processes function in Sweden will
dismiss all likelihood of conspiracy straight away.

But then the N.D. comes up with the jaw-dropping argument that the police acted in this way because the N.D.U.
made use of its "constitutional right to demonstrate."

Just a moment, my young democratic friends. If
the N.D. is going to start evoking the constitution, it is
high time that the party started to abide by it. The party
evidently needs to follow a basic course in law. Sweden upholds the freedom to demonstrate. This freedom
applies to National Democrats, but equally to homosexuals, anarchists, Social Democrats, teenagers and Boy
Scouts. The law is so simple to follow that even a National
Democrat should be able to understand it.

If the N.D.U. wants to demonstrate, all it need do is to
apply to the appropriate authority and request permission
to demonstrate. Pride had the necessary permit from the
police. The N.D.U. did not. There is no support in the constitution for the spontaneous assembly on Slottsbacken of
a gaggle of skinheads with the aim of provoking and inter-
rupting a constitutional activity.

The fact that N.D.U. activists suffer from sexually neu-
rotic disturbances and have problems with gays is not an

issue for either Pride or the constitution. The N.D.U. still
has no right to wave banners urging people to "Crush the
gay lobby."

But above all else the constitution provides no justification whatsoever for the assault on Facundo Unia. He was
the one whose constitutionally protected rights were con-
travened more than anyone else's that Saturday. Facundo
Unia was subjected to a crude and brutal assault for no
reason other than that he was taking part in Pride. It was
not the police, the mass media, established politicians or a
group of lesbians who beat him up. It was the young democrats in the N.D.U.

THE TERROR WE TURN A BLIND EYE TO

Expo no. 1/2003

In the last few decades an unknown number of homosexuals have been murdered, on average one or two per year. Several hundred gay men, lesbians and bisexuals have been subjected to violence, sometimes extreme violence. Thousands have suffered threats of violence, insults, harassment, robbery, or less serious forms of ill-treatment. Premises used by homosexuals have been attacked and destroyed by firebombs.

A form of terrorism is taking place in Sweden that military strategists in the Pentagon usually define as low-intensity warfare. The terminology is taken from guerrilla wars in the Third World where those taking part lack the resources or the political opportunity to conduct a campaign and so resort to pinprick attacks that create fear and confusion.

On another level the terrorists' propaganda troops—Psy-Ops—are active, motivating and rationalizing violence directed at homosexuals. The propaganda takes the form of Internet campaigns, articles, pamphlets and agitational speeches at rallies. The propagandists are identifiable. They include National Democrat leaders who describe homosexuality as a disgusting disease on local radio. Other typical homophobes are the leaders of Nazi organizations such as the Swedish Resistance Movement, Nationalist Youth, Info-14, the National Socialist Front and similar groups.

One thing is clear. Society is not that bothered about this type of low-intensity terrorism. The campaign is aimed at so-called "soft targets"—homosexuals who do not have the resources or are in no position to fight back. Like all bullies, the National Democrats and similar activists prefer to attack from a position of superiority. Stirring up homophobia is fairly risk-free.

Had this hate campaign been aimed at some other representative group of people in Sweden, things would have looked very different. If the targets had been employees of IKEA, bus drivers in Uppsala or members of the Centre Party in Åmål, counter-measures would have been in a quite different category.

If, for instance, five employees of the Ministry of Justice had been murdered and the remainder of their colleagues exposed every day to systematic violence and harassment simply for being civil servants, Sweden would have been in a state of war by now.

The journal *Expo* is now back as an independent magazine after four years as a partner of *Svartvitt* (Black and White). The last issue of *Expo* appeared in the winter of 1997 and was dedicated largely to far-right hate campaigns against homosexuals. So it is appropriate for the first issue of the new *Expo* also to be a special feature on homophobia.

Homophobia—hatred and fear of homosexuals—is a part of the Swedish cultural background. Right-wing extremists are by no means the only ones who stir up hatred of homosexuals. It may well be the commonest cause of fights at parties or in pubs—man-in-the-street Svensson feels provoked by another man's or woman's sexual orientation. But Svensson's inability to handle his sexuality is very different from the homophobia of the extreme right. No other ideology, with the exception of some religious groups, turns homophobia into a watchword.

The hatred of homosexuals by the extreme right is currently enjoying a renaissance. In the postwar years the far right concentrated its attacks on the left, the labor movement, liberalism, feminism and a dozen or so other phenomena.

With very few exceptions extreme-right organizations in the 1950s and 1960s hardly ever used the word "homosexuality" in their publications. When the term did occur, it was in passing, or in connection with some widely publicized incident. As if homosexuality barely existed in those days, the topic plays a fairly subordinate role in their propaganda.

It was only when the gay rights movement began to take off in the 1970s and 1980s and it became more common for homosexuals to come out of the closet and acknowledge their sexual orientation that homophobia once again became a practicable political tool for these groups. And it was only when homophobia became an ideological slogan that systematic violence began.

SVENSKA MOTSTÅNDSRÖRELSEN (SWEDISH RESISTANCE MOVEMENT) —A ZIONIST CONSPIRACY?

www.expo.se
October 24, 2003

We have now reached the point when our astonishment at the nationalist liberation movement's choice of powerful symbols can no longer be silently ignored. The nationalist symbolic language is a constant source of curiosity and surprise. Most jaw-dropping, of course, is the choice of symbol by the Svenska Motståndsrörelsen (S.M.R.— Swedish Resistance Movement)—a lion with a crossbow. Readers are requested to sit up straight and pay attention in order to follow the intricate ins and outs of this story.

Anders Nilsson, one of the leading lights of the S.M.R., is portrayed in the latest edition of *Nationellt Motstånd*

(Nationalist Resistance). Underneath his checked shirt we can make out a tattoo: an armed lion rearing on its hind legs.

Anders Nilsson no doubt knows (or does he?) that he has been branded with an indelible image of one of the most important Zionist and Jewish symbols. Bearing in mind that Nilsson (we suppose) is an educated and enlightened person, we must assume that he is aware of the historical Jewish connotations of this lion. Comrades of a suspicious turn of mind may therefore conclude that Mr. Nilsson is part of the Zionist conspiracy of Z.O.G. agents who have infiltrated the nationalist movement. Why else swagger around displaying such an arch-Jewish symbol?

Let us take this remarkable story from the beginning. The Swedish Resistance Movement and its youth wing, Natio- nell Ungdom (N.U.—Nationalist Youth) were founded in the late 1990s. Among the organization's leading figures are veterans of the old White Aryan Resistance organization, one of the most implacable terrorist branches of Swedish Nazism, whose main purpose was to combat Z.O.G.—a fictitious conspiracy that threatens the very existence and survival of the white Aryan race.

The S.M.R chose a lion with a crossbow as its logo. The symbol featured as the logo for the journal *Folktribunen* (the People's Tribune), recurring in various contexts: on sticky labels, on letter paper and, now, as a tattoo on Anders Nilsson's lower arm. Rumor suggests that several members of the S.M.R. have similar tattoos.

The symbol that Mr. Nilsson takes such pride in goes back thousands of years. From time immemorial, the

Lion of Judah has been one of the Jewish people's most popular and folkloric symbols. In its earliest form it is likely to have been an Old Egyptian symbol, but it was appropriated by the tribe of Judah and taken with them when they emigrated, becoming a dominant feature of history books. King David is descended from the House of Judah, and the lion is regarded as symbolizing Jewish power and God, alternately.

You might think this would be hard for the anti-Jewish Swedish Resistance Movement to swallow. In its earliest manifestation it is likely that Judah's lion was lying down, or standing on all four legs. Remnants of the symbolism appear in the English coat of arms, for instance, but also among the marijuana-smoking Rastafarian movement, which worships Emperor Haile Selassie—better known as the Lion of Judah. Haile Selassie is not mentioned in the Bible, of course, but typical examples of the Ethiopian lion and the lion with the Star of David occur on Rastafarian T-shirts.

At some point in its early history the lion stood on its hind legs, and in that form Judah's lion came to Europe along with emigration during the Roman occupation. Which brings us to late biblical times.

Just over a thousand years ago the symbol accompanied William the Conqueror across the English Channel to become part of the English coat of arms, besides spreading to the Scottish Highlands in the form of the Red Lion or the Celtic Lion. This is when the lion began to acquire its modern guise, in which it appears today over the door of every other pub in Scotland.

The symbol came to Sweden in the fifteenth century, when it was stylized and provided with a crossbow. Since the sixteenth century at least the symbol has been linked with the province of Småland, and also appears on the coat of arms of the provinces of Kronoberg and Kalmar. Another variant was equipped with a Nordic and Oriental sword and became a late Middle Ages Finnish symbol.

And so this is the Jewish symbol that the Swedish Resistance Movement has now stolen in order to stress its anti-Jewish willingness to fight.

What is most side-splittingly funny is that the Swedish Resistance Movement's lion very nearly became the national flag of Israel when it was founded in 1948. The lion standing on its hind legs is intimately linked with the Zionist movement, which emerged towards the end of the nineteenth century, and sure enough a detail in a photograph from the second Zionist World Congress held in Basel in 1898 reveals that the first Zionist flag had a rampant lion in the center of a Star of David. It continued to be their flag until well into the twentieth century, and was one of the candidates in discussions about the new national flag of Israel.

Let us not prolong the pain, but for the comrades in the Zionist . . . excuse me, in the Swedish Resistance Movement, it might be of interest to know that a lot of organizations bid to use the symbolic Lion of Judah. In San Diego, U.S.A., for example, there is a movement called the International Branch of the Lion of Judah. It is an anti-globalization organization with links to the left-wing website Indymedia. Comrade Nilsson should have no difficulty in becoming an honorary member. All he needs to do is to show them his lower arm.

The lion remains one of the most enduring icons of the Zionist movement, and occurs in many contexts and variations. For instance, when the National Democratic Youth Association (N.D.U.) was trying to cobble together a symbol for its patriotic campaign, they chose a lion's head. But once again proud Swedish nationalists slipped up when confronted by the mysteries of heraldry. The N.D.U. chose a symbol that is very similar to that used by the Singapore government, which can be admired on www.gov.sg. The comrade who designed the N.D.U. logo must have spent a long time carefully studying the prototype in Singapore.

In this context it seems relevant to mention that, according to the government of Singapore, the five parts of the lion's mane symbolize democracy, peace, progress, justice and equality. But we shall reveal its background as a symbol of Freemasonry on some other occasion.

However, this is simply not good enough. It is bad enough to note that the nationalist movement lacks originality, but it is humiliating for the N.D.U. to stoop to scraping the bottom of the barrel and importing their logo from Singapore, and for the most fanatical of anti-Jewish groups to need to borrow the central feature of Z.O.G.'s symbolism.

Expo has therefore decided to organize a competition for the general public. The task is to create two genuinely Swedish patriotic symbols that we can offer to the warriors in the S.M.R. and N.D.U. respectively. Entries should be sent by e-mail in jpg form by December 1 at the latest. *Expo* has set up a jury consisting of Professor Moses Abraham, a heraldic specialist at Tel Aviv University, who will be able to attest to the fact that any future S.M.R. logo is free from Jewish influence, and Singapore's representative in the Bilderberg Group,[1] Prime Minister Goh Chok Tong, who will see to it that the N.D.U. symbol is untainted by Illuminati legacies. The winning entry will receive one year's free subscription to *Expo*.

Note

1. The Bilderberg Group is an annual private conference with delegates from North America and Western Europe representing government and politics, finance, industry, labor, education and communications.

9,001 KILOMETRES TO BEIJING

Vagabond—1987

Vagabond's Stieg Larsson and Per Jarl press their noses against the windowpanes in coach 8 of International Express train no. 20 as it glides quickly out of Yaroslavsky in Moscow.

The chaos of the railway station is soon left behind and they pass by dark warehouses like those alongside railway lines all over the world. Soon the last of the lights from Moscow's suburbs are swallowed up by the silent drizzle, and the rat-a-tat-tat from the rails grows louder as the locomotive increases speed.

The journey to Beijing has begun.

We arrived on the Tolstoy express from Helsinki. It was early morning. It was raining.

We stayed for two days. Met Muscovites.

Then began the long journey eastwards on the Trans-Siberian Railway. To Beijing.

Once upon a time, more than a thousand years ago, rebelling peasants in the Volga region trained a bear and sent it to kill the local despot, Prim Yaroslav the Clever.

But the plan misfired.

The revolt collapsed when the prince took up his battle-axe and made short work of the bear. There is no record of what happened to his disloyal subjects, but he had a town built at the location of the incident, named after himself.

Time passed by, and eventually railway trains were invented, and the town of Yaroslavl became the terminus of a stretch of railway line that began in Moscow. It made sense to call the station in the capital Yaroslavsky—the station to Yaroslavl.

When even later the railway network expanded eastwards, they extended the line from Yaroslavl and kept going until they reached Vladivostok. Thus it was that an insignificant prince in the tenth century gave his name to one of the starting points of the world's longest and most heavily used railway.

Moscow is one of the world's most important centers of power. Beijing is another. The distance between the two cities on the Trans-Siberian Railway via Manchuria is 9,001 kilometers. You can cover the distance by airplane in ten hours. By train it takes seven days.

Many people would consider it a serious case of masochism to sit cooped up in a cramped railway carriage for a week without access to a shower or air conditioning or any other of the creature comforts nowadays considered to be essential.

But human beings are travelers, and for professionals among the vagabonds, travelling is a way of life. In a world where flying has become nothing more than streamlined goods traffic, where boats are synonymous with expensive luxury cruises and going by car or coach is something for plebs, rail travel is the only possibility.

And for railway freaks the Trans-Siberian is the classic dream: a journey on the railway to crown all railways.

There were twenty-eight of us who ignored the prophets of doom and made our way to the Yaroslavsky shortly before midnight on July 31.

We had all bought our tickets individually, and pure chance brought us together in coach 8 of International Express train no. 20. We were a mixed bunch of individualists from Scandinavia. Among our number were two taciturn punks from Finland, in the same sleeping compartment as a 66-year-old retired Norwegian sea captain on his way to Shanghai on nostalgic business. And the three musketeers from Lycksele, along with a Norwegian-Israeli chemist and a Dane whom nobody could understand when he spoke, but he was nevertheless a decent bloke. Then there was the lady who opened a nightclub in one of the compartments, and the professional traveler from Stockholm who had prepared himself in meticulous detail. And the young man with ambitions to be a writer, the couple from Börlänge who were complete beginners when it came to travelling, the character with a Hasselblad camera worth 20,000 kronor who intended to stay in the Orient until his money ran out, and the academic couple on their way to a three-month walking holiday in China. Not to mention the conscientious objector from Skåne fleeing to Tibet, and the two Norwegians who intended to fly home the moment they landed in Beijing. And lots more.

No doubt we were a quite typical group of Trans-Siberian travelers.

Travelers have given Yaroslavsky the nickname of the Big Chaos. Not without reason. Train No. 20 chugged quietly in shortly after midnight, twenty minutes before departure time. As it did so the departures screen informed passengers of the relevant platform.

The immediate effect was that about 350 passengers and 900 friends and relatives and porters all started heading in the same direction. Between them and the train were a thousand other passengers waiting for their train, or new arrivals desperately searching for the exit.

The North Koreans seem to be the ones most familiar with how best to proceed. After what we assume must be many years of practice they load their luggage onto trolleys without more ado, then plow their way through the mass of people, completely ignoring anybody in their way. To maximize your chances of catching your train, make sure your travel insurance is up to date, hold onto your luggage for all you are worth, then take your life into your hands and plunge into the wake behind the North Koreans.

Once you have found the right coach and the right sleeping compartment, you will need to decide which of the four bunk beds will be your home for the coming week. A top bunk will be more private—in theory, at least—but a bottom bunk automatically supplies you with a seat next to the window and the little table.

Obeying the deep-rooted instincts of the rail traveler, we fight our way back out into the corridor in order to press our noses against the windowpane when the train starts moving.

Some of the passengers in coach 8 become the best of friends and decide to continue their journey through the Orient together. A few fall out, but are soon reconciled. We play poker, drink vodka, discuss politics and learn several rude songs. We have a serious case of the shits, about twenty bad colds and a blossoming romance between a Gothenburger and a Danish girl.

Love on a train—at least on the Soviet state railways—demands patience and an inventive imagination. You cannot count on any privacy in the sleeping compartments, with people constantly popping in and out. There is always somebody smoking in the corridor, the toilets are neither comfortable nor romantic, and the open platforms between carriages are potentially lethal.

Love on board a train is a distinctly platonic experience. Ecstasy is limited to furtive glances, the holding of hands, and whispered conversations when words are drowned out by the song of the rails.

Nevertheless love is born on trains, and that is no coincidence: the train, more than any other phenomenon of transport, has become an unsurpassed romantic symbol for freedom, dramatic adventures and man's eternal dreams of the future.

Murder on the Orient Express, we decide in our philosophical discussions during the journey, could quite simply never have happened in an airplane. On the other hand, trains are the classical setting for the most dramatic yarns. Where would Jules Verne's *Around the World in Eighty Days* have been if Phileas Fogg had not had a train set to fire up? Graham Greene achieved one of his first successes with the story of Dr. Czinner's perilous journey on the *Stamboul Train* in a chaotic central European setting a few years before the First World War. And would Lord Peter have solved the murder in *Five Red Herrings* if Dorothy L. Sayers had not provided him with a railway timetable?

How many times have we seen Cary Grant sneak into the restaurant in Hitchcock's *North by North-West*? How many times have we seen Ava Gardner or Veronica Lake or Alan Ladd say fare-well in the rain on a deserted railway station platform? In *Bridge over the River Kwai* things are taken one step further and the train becomes the absent main character whose arrival everybody is impatiently awaiting.

There are no classic airlines, but plenty of renowned railways: the Transcontinental between New York and San Francisco, the Mombasa Express from Nairobi, the Shinkansen between Tokyo and Osaka, the milk train between New Delhi and Jaisalmer, the Canadian between Toronto and Vancouver.

They are all classic railway lines, but the undisputed king of them all is the Trans-Siberian.

During the journey the compartment window becomes a screen showing a nonstop seven day-long video film of Greater Russia, sometimes monotonous but often unexpectedly fascinating. From Moscow the track first runs northward in an arc towards the River Volga before straightening out in an easterly direction along the 55th degree of latitude. The track winds its way through plains, taiga and steppe. It crosses over some of the world's mightiest rivers and climbs over rolling hills and high mountains. Scattered along the track—apparently by chance—are a dozen or so old peasant villages that, thanks to the railway, have grown into some of the Soviet Union's biggest and most important towns.

But a journey along the Trans-Siberian Railway is not merely a journey through geography and magnificent countryside. It is above all a journey through the time and space of history, to places where every village and every community has played a role in shaping the present day, and where echoes of heroic deeds and tragedies can still be heard.

The dream of a railway from Europe to the Pacific Ocean was born as a military and political necessity when the tsarist Russian empire tried to consolidate its power in the mid-nineteenth century.

The first sod was cut in 1891, after which the line was extended at irregular intervals over the next fifteen years. Several hundred thousand workers were needed to build the line: furthest east, Chinese and Koreans were recruited at a wage of five kronor per day—if they survived the devastating diseases, starvation and the Siberian winter. To take the line through the most difficult terrain the tsar sent in more than twenty thousand detainees and political prisoners who had been sentenced to exile. For every year they survived, their sentence was reduced by a corresponding time.

The first Trans-Siberian Railway, finished in 1906, ran from Lake Baikal over the border to Harbin in China, and then back into Russia. Even before it was finished it had been the direct cause of the 1904–5 war against Japan, which regarded a railway line built in China by the Russians as a threat to their imperial interests. Japan won the war and the tsar decided that the existing railway should be supplemented with a more northerly line exclusively on Russian territory.

The Bolshevik revolution would have been impossible without the railway: the new line was ready by 1917, just in time for the October Revolution to spread like a burning gunpowder trail from coast to coast. During the subsequent civil war the railway played a major part as the young Soviet state's lifeline, and not unexpectedly some of the bitterest battles were fought in places along the railway line.

Not surprisingly, the restaurant car became the most important gathering point outside our own coach. For the whole of the journey through the Soviet Union we were served by a lone but energetic, powerfully built lady who received our orders with a stern expression on her face. This sternness led to intensive efforts on our part to make her laugh, and bets were laid as to whether this was possible.

Those who thought it was not were defeated just before the finishing line. When we thanked her for her service on the last day of the journey, she paused and gave us a frosty smile.

The food is cheap, and one can eat well for a week on less than 250 kronor, even if one gobbles breakfast, lunch and dinner every day. The menu, which is short and easy to remember, comprises beef stroganoff, beef steak, fish, chicken and borscht.

The train's unpredictable movements can have a dramatic effect in the restaurant car: on one occasion the cook opened the cup-board filled with eggs and bottles of kefir as we were negotiating a curve at 140 kilometers an hour. We had to dig him out with a spade.

The train stops in Kirov, 975 kilometers from Moscow; it is a grey, dreary and boring industrial city with 350,000 inhabitants on the edge of the Urals. The only interesting thing about the city is its name, which it acquired from Sergei Kirov at the end of the 1930s.

Sergei Kirov was a fairly junior party official who owes his historical fame more or less to just one thing: in December 1934 he was murdered in his office by another party member named Nikolaev. Due to jealousy, a private quarrel or political disagreements? Nobody knows. Nikolaev was arrested and executed by firing squad after a summary trial.

The murder, which should have been no more than a historical footnote, became an excuse for Stalin to carry out the most comprehensive purge ever on the Soviet Communist Party. The attack on Kirov was an Anarcho-Trotskyist conspiracy, according to Stalin.

The purge lasted five years, and only two of Lenin's old Central Committee from the revolution survived: Alexandra Kollontay, who was the Soviet ambassador in Sweden and hence out of reach, and Stalin himself. At lower levels thousands of party members disappeared in the terror. Today, the city named after Kirov remains as an obscene monument to the mass murders.

A white obelisk flickers past in the darkness of the night in the Ural Mountains, marking the spot where Europe ends and Asia begins. Nobody could see it properly but we knew it was there and we celebrated the moment by emptying the last drops of the vodka we had bought at the *beriozka* shop in Moscow.

Thereafter, the train is dry.

During the Brezhnev epoch the Russians were well on the way to drinking themselves to death, and when Mikhail Gorbachev came to power one of his first measures was to systematically drain the Soviet Union of strong drink. For the rest of the journey to the Chinese border we saw not a single drop of beer or vodka.

The train stopped at about five o'clock on Sunday morning. Those of us with enough strength to raise our heads and gape out of the window and make a clod-hopping attempt to interpret the Cyrillic letters discovered that we were in Yekaterinburg. The town used to be called Sverdlovsk, and is best known as the place where the tsar was shot in July 1918.

Then we go back to sleep.

After the Urals the train crosses the west Siberian lowlands—undulating plains with kilometer after kilometer of coniferous forest interspersed with hundreds of *kolk-hozes*. When we wake up, something has changed. At first we do not know what it is, then we realize that the colors of the countryside are rather different. After the dull greens of the Urals, a watercolor artist must now introduce shades of burnt umber and sienna yellow. It is pretty, but dry and dusty.

A cloud of fine-grained dust penetrates every chink of our carriage and leaves black stains on our clothes and bed linen. It spreads everywhere, gets stuck in our throats, creeps down into our lungs. We soon find ourselves afflicted by running noses, aching sinuses and dry coughs. We learn that one should never set out on a Trans-Siberian Railway journey without a supply of nose drops, Bisolvon cough mixture and a bottle of window-cleaner.

Attending to your personal hygiene amidst all the dust and in temperatures of twenty-five degrees is a problem in west Siberia. There is a washbasin in the toilets of the traditional railway type—in order to get water you have to press a button, but as soon as you cup your hands to catch the water you have to let go of the button and so the water stops running.

As soon as the train sets off the conductor removes the plugs from all the washbasins so that passengers cannot cheat and fill the basins with water. If you are a practical Boy Scout, you will be able to improvise your own plug. What works best is the screw cap of a vodka bottle and a piece of wrapper from a bar of Fazer chocolate. And if you have drunk all the vodka, you can use the bottle as a primitive shower.

At the point where the railway crosses the mighty River Ob, in the late nineteenth century there was a little commercial outpost with a few thousand resident farmers and hunters. Nowadays this is the location of the city of Novosibirsk, an industrial center with one and a half million inhabitants, the country's biggest opera house and one of the most important ports.

Eh, a port in the middle of Siberia? Yes indeed!

Siberia is pioneer territory with few usable roads. The River Ob flows up from Novosibirsk to the Arctic Ocean, over three thousand kilometers to the north. Thanks to all the tributaries and the Rivers Yenisey and Lena, during the six months of the year that are ice-free it is possible to reach more or less all of Siberia by boat.

If the Third World War ever breaks out, the first American intercontinental missile will land here. This is not only because doing so would wipe out a large part of the Russian defense industry: just outside Novosibirsk is Akademgorodok—the city of knowledge—which is the home of some forty thousand researchers and their families, and hence is where the best brains of Russia are concentrated. This is where the basis of glasnost policies was created, the anti-bureaucratic pioneer spirit. This is where the exploitation of Siberia's enormous natural resources is planned. This is where the future of the Soviet Union is decided.

After Novosibirsk, the train begins the long ascent into the Sayan Mountains. In the city of Krasnoyarsk we cross the River Yenisey and find ourselves in remarkable and majestic countryside—the renowned Russian taiga with its enormous coniferous forests and larch trees, the world's biggest source of timber.

On the edge of the taiga, in Omsk, Fyodor Dostoyevsky was imprisoned at the end of the 1840s, sentenced to four years of exile with repeated horse-whippings. He took his revenge in his auto-biographical novel *The House of the Dead*, a devastating depiction of tsarist Russia.

Lake Baikal is about as big as the Gulf of Bothnia, and the journey around its southern promontory is the high point of our trip. The view is magnificent, and in coach 8 cameras are clicking nonstop as we are presented with one picture-postcard image after the other. After four days cooped up in a train with temperatures around thirty degrees, the ice-blue water is very inviting. Why on earth did we not book tickets that included a stopover here?

Lake Baikal is a nature reserve, but environmental pollution has raised its ugly head even here and threatens to wreak irreparable damage on the unique animal life. But when a pulp mill was constructed on the shore of the lake, furious locals forced the authorities to build a purification plant even bigger than the factory itself, and it produces nothing but pure drinking water. But in the longer term, of course, the lake is vulnerable to exploitation.

To the Siberian locals we must be a peculiar sight—West Europeans flooding into the station buildings looking for vegetables, cigarettes and picture postcards when our train stops for a few hectic minutes.

Dressed in shorts and T-shirts and equipped with dark sunglasses, Walkman portable cassette players and compact cameras, we make the most of the opportunity to loosen up stiff muscles with a quick jog and some strange stretching exercises. Some of us photograph anything that moves, others can never resist the temptation to see how far away from the track they can wander without missing the train—which sets off with no warning signals of any kind. It becomes especially dramatic and entertaining when other trains suddenly turn up and block the way back. On more than one occasion several passengers have been clinging onto the door handles like Uncle Dagobert.

In the little town of Petrovski Zavod, 5,790 kilometers from Moscow, the locals have booked themselves seats in the stalls outside the station in order to observe what we get up to with great interest. They are not disappointed. The first person to jump down from the train is our friend with the Hasselblad camera. He immediately trips up over a sleeper, rescues his camera with an impressively acrobatic maneuver, scrambles to his feet and then trips over the next sleeper.

He is applauded.

It is only when a somewhat high-spirited group from the train tests the limits of hospitality by climbing up onto the local statue of Lenin in order to be photographed that the mood clouds over, and the local police start to look worried.

Vladimir is a sturdy, silent Russian aged about thirty-five. He is a steward, and hence an important person in our daily life. He is the one who makes sure we toe the line, curses at us when we poke our noses into somebody else's business and shepherds us back into our carriage after station stops. He is also in charge of Comrade Samovar bubbling away at the back of the coach, and serves us with tea and coffee.

At the beginning of our journey he does not know a word of English, but after a few days we realize that he understands far more than we thought, and by the end of the journey we have no difficulty at all in communicating.

For seven days he is a central point in our world, and carries out his job with imperturbable composure, no matter what we get up to. The only time his face clouded over was when a drunken Norwegian was having a smoke on the sly and dropped his cigarette behind his mattress, very nearly setting the carriage on fire.

Apart from that, we had a lot of fun together. Like most Russians, he was very reluctant to let himself to be photographed, and it became a sort of game among the camera enthusiasts to persuade him to pose. We had difficulty in getting him to accept a box of Finnish chocolates and some packets of Marlboro when we parted.

Thank you for everything, Vladimir.

The south Siberian steppe is a magical landscape. When we woke up on the fifth morning, there was not a tree in sight for as far as the eye could see, and the steppe's grass-covered hills shimmered in bewitching colors with ultramarine and Payne's grey in the shadows. The only things to break the horizontal line are the telegraph poles and an occasional Oriental cowboy.

The border between the Soviet Union and China is one of the world's most heavily guarded. It was not far from here that the Sino-Soviet conflict heated up, and Russian and Chinese units fired shots at one another over the River Ussuri in 1969. At lunchtime we see the first bunkers and fortresses, a sure sign that we are nearing the border.

Even though for decades foreign spies have been mapping the Russian defenses in detail, all photography is strictly forbidden for several kilometers before the border.

We follow the original Trans-Siberian railway into China. The hours spent at the border station of Zabaykalsk are undramatic and boring, the highlight being standing in a queue for two hours before getting to the bank's currency exchange counter. If you have a few rubles left it is better to avoid the torture and spend the money on a decent dinner in the station restaurant instead.

Were the Sino-Soviet conflict no more than a propaganda war, the Chinese would win hands down. Two kilometers from Zabay-kalsk is the Chinese border town of Manzhouli. The contrasts between them could not have been greater.

The first sight to greet us as we lean out of the train windows is a row of three splendidly attired border guards standing to attention. We gape at one another for a few second, then somebody on the train starts waving and suddenly, to much cheering, the guards burst out laughing and wave back.

The customs officer is a female photographic model who shyly collects our passports and hopes we are feeling well after our long journey, before bidding us welcome to the People's Republic.

An even bigger shock is in store for us on the platform. When *Vagabond*'s photographer, used to the Russian ban on taking pictures, slinks around stealthily with his camera, a Chinese border guard rushes up and offers to help him to set up his tripod so that we can take decent pictures of the station. When he is photographed himself, he looks extremely pleased and thanks our cameraman with a handshake.

The exchange bureau is manned by eight efficient Chinese equipped with mini-computers. The queue is dealt with in fifteen minutes, and meanwhile we are offered tea and biscuits in the waiting room. Exotic music pours out of the loudspeakers and in the shops, for the first time since leaving Moscow, we can buy beer, vodka and Chinese whiskey. Be warned about the latter: it smells of aviation fuel, and tastes like it, too.

The stay in Manzhouli leaves a surrealistic impression in our memories. Needless to say, much of it is pure window dressing. The Chinese are well aware of how we feel after six days on Russian mineral water and a few incredibly boring hours on the Russian side of the border. Our reception is a stroke of genius in the propaganda war, and there is no doubt that the Chinese win the hearts of most passengers. The barren Siberian steppes are gradually replaced by Chinese maize fields as we cruise down from the highlands into fertile Manchuria. A fantastic journey is nearing its end.

While we are still sorting out our impressions of the Soviet Union the train stops in Harbin, where we say farewell to the Trans-Siberian Railway on which we have been travelling for over eight thousand kilometers. The line continues to Vladivostok, but our tickets are for a final diversion to the south.

At 6.36 the following morning, the last lap is completed and the journey ends just as suddenly as it began when we pull into Beijing Central Station. We have 9,001 kilometers of track behind us, and according to the timetable we are only four minutes late.

The adventure is over, and a new one—among eight million cyclists—awaits us.

STIEG LARSSON, born in 1954, was a journalist. He was the editor-in-chief of *Expo* from 1990, and had previously worked at a major news agency for many years. He was one of the world's leading experts on anti-democratic, right-wing extremist and Nazi organizations, and was often consulted on that account. He died suddenly and unexpectedly in November 2004, soon after delivering the manuscripts for three crime novels to his Swedish publisher. These novels make up the Millennium Trilogy, and have gone on to sell many millions of copies worldwide.

LAURIE THOMPSON is the distinguished translator of the novels of Henning Mankell, Håkan Nesser and Åke Edwardson. He was editor of *Swedish Book Review* between 1983 and 2002.

DANIEL POOHL has been editor-in-chief of *Expo* magazine since 2005.

TARIQ ALI is a writer and filmmaker. He has written more than two dozen books on world history and politics, and seven novels (translated into over a dozen languages), as well as scripts for the stage and screen, and is an editor of *New Left Review*.